THE EMILY DICKINSON READER

The
Emily
Dickinson
Reader

An English-to-English Translation
of Emily Dickinson's Complete Poems

by

Paul Legault

M^CSWEENEY'S

SAN FRANCISCO

www.mcsweeneys.net

Note: The poem numbers herein correspond to the R. W. Franklin edition.

Design by Walter Green and Adam Krefman.
Endpapers by Sunra Thompson. Author photo by Billy Merrell.

McSweeney's and colophon are registered trademarks of McSweeney's,
a privately held company with wildy fluctuating resources.

ISBN: 978-1-936365-98-2

Printed by 1010 Printing International Ltd., China.

…terribler
Like a Panther in the Glove

EMILY DICKINSON

TRANSLATOR'S NOTE

"She was much too enigmatical a being for me to solve in an hour's interview, and an instinct told me that the slightest attempt at direct cross-examination would make her withdraw into her shell; I could sit and watch, as one does in the woods; I must name my bird without a gun, as recommended by Emerson."

        —T. W. Higginson, on first meeting Emily Dickinson

Born on December 10, 1830, in Amherst, Massachusetts, Emily Dickinson is both the father of American poetry and the most infamous lesbian vampire of the nineteenth century.

She wrote 1,789 poems in her lifetime, the bulk of which remained unpublished until her (supposed) death in 1886, when her younger sister Lavinia found them in a trunk. After escaping their Pandoran chamber, Dickinson's works emerged into the twentieth century like an apocalyptic army of angels made entirely of paper.

Emily Dickinson wrote in a language all her own, thus the need for this English version of what she meant. The translations presented here are my attempt to rewrite her poems (with their foreign beauty intact) in "Standard English."

The great Dickinsonian scholar and editor R. W. Franklin[1] writes:

Like every previous appearance of Dickinson's poems, this edition is based on the assumption that a literary work is separable from its artifact, as Dickinson herself demonstrated [...] There can be many manifestations of a literary work.

Seriously. He's right. And this one is personal.

If Emily Dickinson were a church, I would be inside of her right now, writing this. If she were a bee, I would buy a flower costume. If she were still alive, I would attempt, and inevitably fail, to be her best friend. (Maybe we'd hang out sometimes. Though she probably wouldn't visit. Or go online that much.) Instead, I've settled on being her humble translator.

I meant to begin this introduction with a traditional invocation of the Muse(s). Here, one might call upon some of Dickinson's favorites: death, Jesus, sex, bobolinks, her love-interest/sister-in-law Sue,[2] &c. If they'll allow it, I invite *them* now to conclude this preface.

O Great Bobolink, reveal your true song.

O Zombie Mother, explain this book for me—

Emily Dickinson used to exist. Now she's doing it again.

---

1. Editor, *The Poems of Emily Dickinson* (Harvard University Press, 1999)
2. See Index: *Dickinson, Susan Gilbert*; *Sex, Imaginary*; *Incest*

~

1.

Everything has to love something.

2.

Hey, really historically important people.
Guess what? You're all dead.

3.

Life is like a little boat on a sea of itself.

4.

The arrival of spring is somewhat sexually charged.

5.

I am in love with my brother's girlfriend. I am as fond of
her as I am of my younger sister, though I do not want to have
sex with my younger sister. My brother's girlfriend's name
is Sue, and I want to have sex with her.

6.

I'm kind of like a little boat in the sea of life.
Who wants to have sex with its brother's girlfriend.

7.

If you're a flower, I'm your zombie gardener.

8.

Dig up my grave, would you? I'm a zombie,
and I've got some flowers for you!

9.

If today is opposite day, I'm happy.

10.

I could probably only be queen in a completely imaginary state. Otherwise, I don't think the country would do so well culturally or economically, because I would probably appoint plants, specifically roses, into key political and religious offices.

11.

If you pick a rose, it can no longer access water and other vital nutrients that it needs to live.

12.

I lost something that seems to be easily replaceable, but it is not easily replaceable.

13.

I can't wait for this great time when things will really be great. I think this time probably won't occur until I'm dead.

14.

This really is too much.

15.

I woke up this naked woman under a tree, and she was excited to see me. Unfortunately, her name was not Sue.

16.

Good things can come from bad things or situations.

17.

I don't own that many things.

18.

Sue left this morning. She cannot speak to me, because
she is not in the room with me anymore. I cannot speak to her,
because she is not in the room with me anymore!

19.

Do flowers go to heaven when they die?
I guess probably. By flowers, I mean me.

20.

Why didn't you tell me that someone important
to me died, Philip? Jesus.

21.

If autumn is kind of like a parade, then flowers are like
the people who found out about the parade and didn't approve
of the parade, mostly because they weren't invited to be in it,
and then tried to cancel the parade.

22.

A girl died. A bobolink was there.

23.

Birds exist. Bumblebees also exist.

24.

The Earth rotates at about 465 meters per second.
At two points in the day, when the sun is closest to the
horizon, its light is refracted by the Earth's atmosphere,
producing a wide variety of colors in the light.

25.

I wonder what it would be like to be a rose.
No, I am one. And it's great!

26.

Sometimes it snows or sleets. But I'm dead, so I don't care.
Hell, I feel like singing. Zombies can sing too.

27.

There are ghosts in the meadow. I don't really know what to do.

28.

It's opposite day again. And we just won the jackpot.

29.

My dress is too big.

30.

Phenologically speaking, you can tell it's spring by the
blossoming of a range of plant species, and the activities of
animals or the special smell of soil that has reached the temperature
for microflora to flourish. And it is spring.

31.

Some flowers can't grow in swamps.
Orchids can grow in swamps.

32.

It is autumn, and I'm going to put on some earrings.

33.

I don't know where my boat is. Sometimes I go out to the bay to
look for it. It could be anywhere! Because I don't own a boat.

34.

One of my friends died. All of the dead are somewhere together.
It is not really a place I guess.

35.

I woke up before the sunrise.

36.

I am so glad that the economy exists. If I were to die,
I think I would like that it keeps going.

37.

I don't know why I'm smiling. Something is happening in the dark
to make me smile. Possibly this thing is oral sex with Sue.

38.

Sunsets are kind of like treasures. If someone wanted
to share my treasure I wouldn't kill him like if he wanted
the whole thing in which case I'd kill him.

39.

God keeps taking my things. Eventually he gives them back,
but it's really frustrating.

40.

A lot of animals and inanimate objects don't know that I'm
eventually going to die. I don't know how to break it to them.
I think I'll go on a walk with them and then break it to them.

41.

There's this really creepy village over there. It doesn't move very
much. It's probably Death. If Sue dies, I will implode.

42.

I really hate this one word. The word is: "forgot."
There's something about it that gives me the creeps.

43.

There were some kids walking home and everything wanted to
have sex with them. And it creeped them out.

44.

There's this guy that comes around knocking on people's doors
around six thirty or so each day, wearing this red and gold fur-lined
cape. I think he's homeless and sleeps down by the lake sometimes.
Or else he's the sunset.

45.

Look at all these snowflakes! I feel like dancing!

46.

I've been stalking someone. It's great. I have their coat.
I can still smell them on it. Sometimes I cry when I'm smelling it.

47.

The great events of our time are engendered by
the anonymity of their constituents.

48.

Whose face is this?
Oh, it's a dead person's face.

49.

My friend Katie has two legs, which are
attached to her body.

50.

Death doesn't surprise me. Unless it's my own death,
in which case I would probably be surprised.

51.

I love summer! I just love it.

52.

If God were a soldier, he would be a pretty good soldier.

53.

If you want me to stop carrying roses,
you'll have to pry them from my cold, dead hands.

54.

I forget everything else but flowers
when I'm looking at flowers. *Flowers*.

55.

Small things can be very important.
Acorns, for example. Think about it.

56.

I love you. I love everything that you give to me.
Even if it's an arrow and now I'm dead, Sue.

57.

Someone just robbed the forest.
Who the hell would do something like that?

58.

I hate Mondays.

59.

I could be someone who does things.
There are people doing things on a boat over there
that are better things than what I am doing here on the shore.
They happen to be dead people. I wish they would invite
me to their zombie boat parties.

60.

I'm sending you a rose. I would've liked to be this rose
so that you'd put me on your table where I would slowly
run out of nutrients and die right there in the middle
of your kitchen.

61.

Tides cause changes in the depth of marine and estuarine
water bodies and produce oscillating currents known as tidal
streams, making the prediction of them important for coastal
navigation. I am not very good at topographical navigation—
which includes coastal navigation. Some other people are
good at topographical navigation. But I am not. I am not
arriving at the place I was trying to get to because of this.

62.

There's something in here. I think it's a fairy.

63.

Eventually, I will die. No, really, I promise.

64.

I have affections toward a man that I would like to forget. I find it
difficult to forget the affections that I have toward this man.

65.

Noah's dove is like Christopher Columbus. Noah's dove is like
Columbus because it was on a boat kind of like how Columbus was
on a boat, and neither of them wanted to be on a boat anymore, so
they were relieved when they weren't on a boat anymore.

66.

I met this girl who had magical powers.
Actually, I probably just dreamt that.

67.

If she had known how great it is to be dead, she wouldn't have
frowned so much when she was dying. If she hadn't done that, then
her dead body wouldn't have such a sad-looking face on it.

68.

The sky doesn't really move.
But that's not entirely true. The sky kind of moves.

69.

I picked some flowers. But I didn't pick all of the flowers.

70.

There was this woman who was hiding from me.
I found her and kidnapped her. Actually, she was a flower.

71.

I don't really understand what life is.
It does things which are similar to what other things do,
but, ultimately, it is not one of those things that does things
which are similar to the things that it does.

72.

It's my birthday!

73.

There are angels everywhere. *Everywhere.*
There's one on your face.

74.

Instead of flowers, I'm holding a bouquet of eyes, which are
attached to long stalks, kind of like snails' eyes. All the eyes ever
want to talk about is death. I'm okay with that.

75.

Excuse me, pastor, could you tell me where God's bed is?
I need to have sex with Him.

76.

Rainbows and flowers do not have the capacity to use
language for their purposes. Still, *I can hear them.*

77.

Dying is like being in a parade.
Except that at the end of the parade you die.

78.

I can't stop looking at this dead person.
It's as if I won a prize, and it's this dead person. Wonderful.

79.

There are some children running around out back, and
this guy is hanging out in a tree watching them. Oh, wait,
those aren't people at all. Those are birds. And it's spring.

80.

This flower is a symbol of my affection toward you.

81.

Once there was this girl who had it really hard off.
Then she died. *Finally*.

82.

There's something about this flower in particular.
It reminds me of flowers in general. Also of bees.
Also of other things, such as sex *with my brother's girlfriend*.

83.

You can't chase something if it's already dead.

84.

There was this girl who had beautiful feet who doesn't
have feet anymore, because she is dead.

85.

Why is the field covered with these miniature beds?
There are so many miniature-person-sized beds in this field.
I don't know. I wish I was smaller. And Sue was too.

86.

We should behave more like birds.
Chirp. Chirp, chirp.

87.

I feel the same way Jesus did that time when
people wouldn't accept him for who he was.

88.

Some guy walked by my window the other night, whistling.
I'm feeling kind of down these days. I kind of hope he walks
by again, and he's whistling. Or else he has a trumpet this time,
and he's playing the trumpet.

89.

When I'm restless, there are all these angels who want me and all
these demons who want me and suddenly everything wants me.

90.

Happy St. Nicodemus Day.

91.

Sometimes people get really fragile, and then they die.
But that's okay—death has all kinds of treasures. Its treasures
include: dead children, dead birds, dead farm animals…

92.

This is my flower. You can borrow it, but you better damn well give
it back. There is something sexual about this exchange.

93.

Everything is metamorphosed into its opposite to
perpetuate itself in its expurgated form.

94.

Is there a creek inside of the muscle that pumps blood
through your circulatory system at which woodland creatures
go to drink? I'm just curious.

95.

Flowers understand ecstasy much better than we humans do.
Silly humans.

96.

Instead of being an English duchess, I think I'd rather be a crazy
person who lives in the woods and runs around naked or else only
wears things that she's put together from different leaves and
grasses, and I'll eat what I catch with my hands, and I will ambush
all who pass, and I will be beautiful in the woods with my army of
bees, and they will call me "The Queen of the Forest!"

97.

God, your angels are really sassy.
I asked them a question, and they gave me a lot of attitude.

98.

Here are some flowers, Sue. Again. Come on, just take them.

99.

After solving a problem, there is often another
problem that you need to solve.

100.

What kind of hotel is this?
It's really cold, there's no one at the bar, there's not
even a desk clerk. Oh wait, this isn't a hotel at all. It's death.

101.

God took some of my stuff again. This is my stuff, God.
I'm going to sue you.

102.

All the royalty here wear really shoddy clothes.
That's just their thing. It's a shoes-off kind of household.

103.

If I could, I would kill everybody, and after I was done
killing everybody, I'd commit suicide.

104.

I like summer. I like all kinds of things about summer.
What else. Wizards are tireless creatures. They never sleep.

105.

People get really worked up about death. Get over it.

106.

She has this glow-in-the-dark hat. Also, her dress glows in the dark.
Also, her face does. Also, she's actually the sun.

107.

For some reason, I remind people of Germany.

108.

I have a very strong imagination. For example, say
I imagine that I'm in the Alps. Oh, it's very nice here in the
Alps. The Alps are very high, here in the Alps. Goodness, how
did I get to the Alps? And who am I anyway? Oh, yes, I'm a daisy.
I'm a daisy in the Alps…

109.

You win some, you lose some.

110.

Flowers grow from ugly things called bulbs.
Butterflies also come from ugly things. This perplexes me.

111.

There's paint all over the place.
It looks like a couple of painters got into a fight and
got paint all over the place. Actually, it's a sunset.

112.

You only want what you can't have.
That's why dying people are so sad.

113.

This place is really great. Oh, wait. Damn it. Am I dead?

114.

Welcome to Heaven. We have a few rules here:
1. No bells before twelve o'clock.
2. No zombie children allowed.
3.All the male gymnasts must stay indoors.
(I don't make the rules, I just follow them.)

115.

Dead people aren't very ambitious. They're also
not very affectionate. The only thing dead people have going
for them is that they'll never die.

116.

Again. You win some, you lose some.

117.

Classification denies the immediate experience.

118.

If you brag too much, someone might try to kill you.

119.

You call this dying? This is nothing. Turn it up a notch.

120.

I want heaven as much as a thirsty person wants water.
Which is a lot.

121.

I can't give you pearls or fancy hats. I can, however, build a nest inside
your heart where I will return once a year to live inside of you, Sue.

122.

It's late winter/early spring. It's kind of warm, but not that
warm. Like purgatory. Summer, why don't you invite all the
neighborhood kids over to get drunk with you already?

123.

It's winter. Someone is going around touching people in the eye.
Mostly he or she has been touching short people in the eye.
If you're not very tall, you should probably watch out.

124.

Mary and the apostles don't care about planetary movements.
Or the politics of Venice. They don't even care about hats.
Because they're dead. And they live in this really great house.
It's a very sturdy and well-furnished house.

125.

Once there was this body part just lying on the side
of the road. God sent down some angels to pick it up
and bring it up to Heaven. It's better off there. There are a lot
of boats in Heaven. Everything likes boats.

126.

I like to roofie people.

127.

Flowers are similar to human children.

128.

I'm dead. Just kidding—I'm not really dead.
I'm glad I'm not really dead like those dead people that they buried.

129.

Italy is much nicer than Switzerland.

130.

There are these baby birds who are alone because their mother
died. Actually, they're not entirely alone, because, though
she's dead, their mom can still see them from up in Heaven.
And now she has to watch as each of them slowly dies.

131.

Be yourself. That's my motto. I just happen to be immortal.

132.

I was finally having a good time, and then I died. Next time that
I'm alive—which will be never—I will try to enjoy myself
more thoroughly.

133.

Jesus, let me inside of your fur coat. It is big enough
that you can let me in, and I can fall asleep there, and no one
will ask you: what's that you got there, under your coat?
Or if someone does, I'll pop my head out and tell them what
my name is, very quietly, so they won't necessarily be able to
hear what I said, and then I'll go back inside.

134.

Once you have sex with someone, they usually don't
want to have sex with you as much as they did before you
had sex with them. Hi, Sue.

135.

The average human can survive a long time on very little food.
I hope that's all you want. Because that's all you're getting.
Back in your cage!

136.

Zombies have it really hard off. That's why they appreciate
kindness more than other people.

137.

It's spring! So how come all the trees aren't screaming with delight?
Maybe they don't have mouths.

138.

My suffering is greater than the suffering of entire armies.

139.

Houses should be warm. Otherwise, what good is a house?

140.

Someone, get me a drink. And some poetry.
I want to know what life is about.

141.

She frolicked herself to death. Now she haunts that hill over
there—frolicking. Her ghost-body is made of evaporated water.

142.

As with other types of pupae, the chrysalis stage in most butterflies
is one in which there is very little movement. Within the chrysalis,
growth and differentiation occur. The adult butterfly emerges
from this and expands its wings by pumping hemolymph into the
wing veins. This sudden and rapid change from pupa to imago
is called metamorphosis.

143.

I enjoy seeing the ocean because I don't ever see the ocean.

144.

I relate to people who have been in prison.
I'm in prison, figuratively.

145.

After wrestling with Jacob all night, the angel suggested they
get breakfast. But Jacob wanted more than just breakfast.
And he got it. Take that, God.

146.

The nightingale is a migratory bird that nests in climate zones in
which the average temperature during growing season is something
close to fifteen degrees Celsius.

147.

In modern science, a representative individual
can be used to illustrate universal truths about its species.
In this way, everything exists in plurality.

148.

It's nighttime and I forget what morning looks like.
Does it have feet? It probably doesn't have feet,
but I think I remember it having feet.

149.

Caesar, get off your high horse and take that poor girl's flower.
I don't care if it's just a daisy. Or if you don't like her father.
Or if you're dead.

150.

Daffodils are really great. I prefer them to most humans.
Except Sue.

151.

God, we must look like small, insignificant animals to you.

152.

My boat sank. Luckily, I'm only referring to a paper boat
or a leaf or something that I imagined as a boat. But for all
the people that died on that imaginary boat—how they drowned
and how it was horrible—death is a real thing.

153.

You call this corruption? I like it.

154.

She died. She died because her vital organs failed,
stopping the blood flow to her brain and other tissues,
leading to their deterioration.

155.

Pain prepares us for joy. In that case,
whatever comes next is going to be awesome.

156.

Surgeons must be very careful.

157.

If I don't get enough sleep, I can be really grumpy the next day.

158.

You know my friends are dead when I'm wearing black.

159.

She was dying, and then all of a sudden she was dead.
It took a few months. I noticed a change in the seasons.

160.

Don't look so glum. People might think you're pessimistic.

161.

Daisies are phototropic.

162.

I think I'm hallucinating. Yes, I'm confident of it.
There are as many robins as points in the sky that form a
grid from which spring exists.

163.

My poems are overwrought.

164.

Today isn't just charming. It's übercharming.

165.

I'm passive-aggressive. I hold my emotions in, so when they do
come out, they destroy everything in their path, and they will
destroy you, and you should probably run, or I will destroy you.

166.

Death is a bastard. He is not very affable and has a
hard time making friends. Even Jesus doesn't like him.
Jesus doesn't like him one bit.

167.

Happiness is a little obsessed with itself.

168.

If I were a witch, I would ask my secret wizard friend
to teach me how to instill an irremovable pain in people I
don't like. Really, I just want everybody to love me. Really,
I just think everyone should love me or else suffer.

169.

Martyrs are better than living people, because they
get to wear really good clothes now that they're dead, and
they get to hang out with angels, and when God passes
them on the street, sometimes he lifts his hat to them and
wishes them a good afternoon.

170.

I have experienced a bliss that cannot be approximated in
qualitative terms, such that no misery can matter against the fact
that it was. I might compare it to a gun at sea—this is to
say, to a fierce yet specific tool whose use gives a geography
to the vastness that surrounds it by the sound which travels out into
that endlessly horizontal terrain, like a bell, that was bliss, or the
sound of a bell that was, and in stopping, seems to create
the silence out of which it came to exist.

171.

I have a secret: caterpillars eventually turn into butterflies.

172.

The sun has risen. I can see farther than I can walk.

173.

This flower is insignificant. Except for the personal
and daily reasons other possibly insignificant beings give
to justify its existence.

174.

Portraits evoke a nostalgia that is lacking in the actual
subject that is portrayed.

175.

I have tried to store my life away as if it were a material
thing that could be stored. I put it in a barn. But it's not there
anymore. It was right here in this barn.

176.

I want something to the point of desperation.
I will kill things for it. Its name is Sue.

177.

There's this thing that is as great as leaving the cold familiarity of
everyday life for a pleasure garden in which your senses compete to
be the one to master you. That thing is sex.

178.

Divinity can only exist as an absence.

179.

God prefers stupid people.

180.

I have some really steamy love letters that I keep inside of this
black box. I have some flowers that I keep inside of this box too.
Also some hair.

181.

I'm into dominant-submissive relationships and the pleasures that
are intricately connected to pain.

182.

I have been hallucinating again.

183.

I met some royalty today. I'm certain they were royalty, though
they dressed like peasants. They weren't even wearing shoes.
Or else I met some poor people today.

184.

Love has really big hands.

185.

I have either lost my virginity or died between the hours of
midnight and six in the morning. It is unclear which.

186.

Some homeless people juggle in the streets to make money.

187.

It's tough being a martyr.

188.

Martyrs are consumed by the act of representing the ideal human
being. In this way, they are no longer human. In this way, they are
useless, except as guides on how to be martyrs.

188.

Do you mind if I close this door?

189.

Sue, I would like to be alone with you.

190.

I am not a flower or a bird, but I have experienced feelings that
I associate with being flowers and birds.

191.

Everyone has morning activities. Farmers have to farm.
Dying people have to die. Brides have to marry into unhappy
relationships. That we must believe in God is cruel.

192.

It's really great when two people who love each other die
at the same time. Really, it's just fantastic!

193.

Sometimes when I am sad I stay completely still.

194.

Have you seen my husband? I can't seem to find him.
His name is Jesus.

195.

I am small and not very good at many things. That said,
I'm really good at starving to death.

196.

My boss is mad at me, so I'm going to send him a feather in the mail
in the hopes that he will receive said feather and not be mad at me
anymore. I think this is a good plan.

197.

Jesus, I hope you learned your lesson when you got crucified.
It's hard work being human.

198.

You should teach your baby to say my name.

199.

I like to arrive fashionably late so that everyone who has
been waiting for me, in agony, for what seems like decades, turns
to see me, desperate to experience all that is me and the full
glory of my entrance.

200.

I noticed a woman acting strangely. I think it was because she was in love. I think it was because she was in love with Sue. I think she was me.

201.

Because of your absence, I have turned into a feral cat. Finally.

202.

Science has more practical uses than religion.

203.

I like it when I only almost know something.

204.

I saw the sunrise this morning. Let me tell you about it. It was fantastic.

205.

I want you to make love to me slowly but entirely.

206.

I am shy around you, because I like you.

207.

I just did ecstasy for the first time. It reminded me of the first time I got drunk. It also reminded me of that time when I reeled through endless summer days from inns of molten blue. You know. That time.

208.

Birds nest in trees.

209.

I can't find the Earth. Have you seen it? You'd probably
recognize it. It's big and made up of large bodies of water
with a few scattered landmasses.

210.

When I'm dead, I probably won't move. But if I could move,
I'd move my dead mouth to say "Thank you." I'd also remind
you to feed my pet bird, now that I'm dead. Thanks.

211.

I like organ music.

212.

God keeps the Holy Ghost inside of a cage.

213.

I don't keep up with gossip.

214.

It's okay that everyone forgot about me. Really, I'm fine.

215.

Jesus has a lot of explaining to do.

216.

A woman died last night. It is very pretty this morning.
Except that she's dead.

217.

I find it hard to explain myself.

218.

You say you love me but you better damn well be sure of it.

219.

I have this river. In some cases, a river flows into the ground
or dries up completely before reaching another body of water.
I hope this is not the case with my river.

220.

Every human action is a small thing that leads ultimately to death.

221.

This one time I spent the night with this guy, and the next morning
he had to go but didn't want to. I also had to go but didn't really
want to. So we just sat around together instead. And it was nice.

222.

Oh no, I'm dying. Where's Jesus when you need him? Oh, wait,
forget Jesus, here comes my brother's girlfriend, Sue, who I'm
in love with. Dying's not so bad when she's around. Maybe I'm not
even dying. Maybe I have a cold and am being dramatic about it.

223.

The best time to eat corn is at noon.

224.

Nighttime is horrible.

225.

It's really "great" being a wife.

226.

I stole these flowers from a bee. He seemed okay with it.

227.

I saw this one guy drown this other guy. The victim was flailing
his arms. The murderer smiled at me. I don't know why I didn't
report it to the police.

228.

I want more than I can emotionally capacitate.

229.

There's music everywhere, though most of the music
is dead people music.

230.

When I am dead, I will miss that there are trees.

231.

My best friend's name is Tim. I will just die if he ever dies.
And if I die first, Tim better do the same for me.

232.

I told you so.

233.

Let me tell you how to paint a sunset. You have to start with
some blue, and just a little bit of gray, and some gold.
Then put some red pants on it.

234.

I don't want to leave my friend, because he might die
while I'm gone, and then I would be heartbroken, and I hate
being heartbroken.

235.

One must be able to turn down sexual
propositions gracefully, Sue.

236.

I don't go to church. I am the church.

237.

There is a dog that lives inside of my heart who is
desperate for your attention.

238.

Zombies are similar to robots.

239.

It's summer! Just kidding. Actually, it's winter.

240.

There are miseries greater than human miseries that
cannot be experienced.

241.

Everyone gets new shoes in Heaven.

242.

It is hard for me to get things done when I am upset.
For example, sometimes where my hand should be, there is instead
a large predatory cat. At these times, it is hard to put on gloves.

243.

It doesn't take much to make me think of death.

DICKINSON, THINKING ABOUT BIRDS.

244.

I'm an alcoholic, figuratively speaking.
Figuratively, I want to drink myself to death.

245.

I was playing with someone, and then he died, and then
it wasn't fun anymore.

246.

The morning is jealous of the afternoon because
of that two timing tramp the Sun.

247.

Parasites inhabit living organisms and therefore face problems
that free-living organisms do not. Hosts generally try to avoid,
repel, and destroy parasites. In the case of one's soul, a type of
parasite often transmitted at birth, the body gives up. The body is
a slave to the soul, which ultimately has no use for it.

248.

I want to spend my life on my life.

249.

Heaven is a popular cliché. Hell is interesting.

250.

I do not trust the justice system.

251.

Things could be worse to the point at which they could not be
worse which is when I am not with you.

252.

When I'm an angel I'm going to be a really
sexy angel who looks like Sue.

253.

I keep bringing these things that nobody wants.
Does anybody want these? No? Alright.

254.

Men like women. I guess I don't mean *just* men.

255.

If I am a small, insignificant thing, and God is everything,
then I am a small, insignificant thing named God.

256.

I'm not very worldly. I'm kind of New Englandy.

257.

All this is a little silly. All this that I'm doing.

258.

I want to buy your face. I have all these diamonds and
I want you to trade me these diamonds for your face.
Actually, I really just want the mouth part of your face.

259.

This clock is really broken. There's no way to fix this clock.
This is similar to the way you can't fix things like dead people.

260.

I'm so insignificant that I don't even exist. I'm so insignificant that I don't even want to exist. I don't even want people to know that I don't exist. The way frogs exist. And no one cares about them. The way they're arrogant the way they exist. I hate frogs.

261.

The problem with memory is how it makes me feel stupid.

262.

Who cares about aeronautics? Death is the only way to travel.

263.

Jesus doesn't care if he doesn't live at someone's house, he'll just go inside anyway and do whatever he pleases without them knowing it, because he's sneaky like that.

264.

I have the same brain and the same body and the same circulatory system as someone else who is me who I don't even know.

265.

It's not summer or spring or winter.
What could it be? Oh. Probably it's autumn.

266.

You know I'm all in when I say that I'll bet my biggest bobolink on it. Trust me.

267.

When I die, everyone will finally find out my big secret.
(I'm actually a man.)

I don't think they'll let me into Heaven, because I'm a talker.
Probably people who talk too much should go to Hell.

The nights can no longer sustain themselves on the domestic alone.
In fact, they will have none of that. In fact, every domestic item
must be put aside and be replaced by the organic version of said
item. In fact, every domestic item must be replaced not just by
any corresponding organic item but with a version of itself that
corresponds to itself on the human body. And this is to say not just
on any body, but yours. And this is to say that the ports must be
replaced with human ports. And the ocean itself should be your
body's ocean. And oral sex is not enough. I would also like to put
my fingers inside you in every configuration. And all of this is to
say that we are not together. But if we were together, the nights
would no longer be the nights that are made up by the course of the
sun over the course of the Earth but would be the nights made from
the course of you over the course of me in bed with you making
love to me thoroughly as to destroy all the objects of which we
have grown tired and which we must transform into these human
objects that you will place over me as I enter Sue entirely.

I'm not a morning person.

If I had premarital sex my moral conscience would be
compromised. God has premarital sex all the time.

272.

Anything you could possibly want, I've got it.
I'm kind of like a corner store.

273.

It's cool to have spina bifida. Jesus had spina bifida.

274.

I went on this walk with this one guy, and it was really nice,
and then we had sex, and then I felt bad about it, so I killed
myself to make him feel bad about having sex with me.

275.

If you die for me, I'll tell God to let you into Heaven.
We're close.

276.

I'm different.

277.

I'm really intense about my written correspondence.

278.

There is something really nice about the human voice.

279.

I really like my soul.

280.

I got married. My husband expects feminine ideals from
me that I cannot deliver. It is all very sad and very serious.
(That's why I didn't really get married.)

281.

You cannot force me to change.
Sunsets can force me to change.

282.

By practicing with inexpensive media one learns
how to handle expensive media.

283.

Sure, we shouldn't have crucified Jesus,
but it all worked out in the end.

284.

I learned about the extreme from the extreme.

285.

Love is nothing compared to überlove.

286.

I was supposed to meet the duke of something,
but I was poorly dressed for the occasion.
It was kind of embarrassing.

287.

It's hard for me to tell the difference between one
abstraction and another. I think I'm in life with you.
Or maybe I'm just in love. Or maybe I'm dead.

288.

I cannot measure the benefits of life against the benefits
of death. I need an accountant.

289.

I like elephants. I like how things don't really bother them.
If they get their feet wet, or step on some thorns, it's not really
a big deal to them, because they're elephants. They're like:
whatever, I'm an elephant.

290.

Let someone else whine about the crucifixion of Jesus.
I say hurry up and do it already.

291.

Snow is a type of precipitation formed from crystalline water
ice, consisting of a multitude of snowflakes that fall from clouds.
Since snow is composed of small ice particles, it is a granular
material. It has an open and therefore soft structure, unless packed
by external pressure.

292.

I was really into this guy, but now I'm over him. Actually, I'm still
really into him. I'm just lying to myself.

293.

I wish that I had lots of hands instead of just two. I would use
my extra hands to press my soul into my body, so that it couldn't
leave, so I wouldn't have to die anymore.

294.

I can imagine a pain so entire that it takes on a person's own
being and starts going by that person's name and running that
person's errands and being that person on a daily basis.
It's name is Emily Dickinson.

295.

God, are you sure you can handle me?

296.

Whatever I imagine, however thoroughly I imagine it, will stop.

297.

California is a really nice place.

298.

Suicidal people enjoy life, because it reminds them of how great
it will be to finally kill themselves.

299.

I can't get over this guy even though he told me to get over him.
Because I'm stupid.

300.

When they finally crucify me, it'll be great! There will be
a parade and everything.

301.

It's my birthday again. I feel old.

302.

The best part about life is how it ends.

303.

At any given moment, there are small, naked people sitting quietly
in the room with me, watching me, constantly,
like sleepless gnomes. In fact, they're here right now.
In fact, I'm probably schizophrenic.

304.

It is hard to accomplish something you set out to accomplish.

305.

I do what I want.

306.

People like you better when you're in a good mood.
Fuck them. I'm in a bad mood.

307.

Rapture's not as good as the idea of rapture.

308.

Breathing is both voluntary and involuntary!

309.

You can kill humans, but you can't stop them from enjoying it.

310.

I don't like real things. I like fake things that are real.
Like my relationship with Sue.

311.

I like to break into people's houses to steal things
when they're asleep. Sometimes I just steal their spoons and
a Crock-Pot or something.

312.

Sometimes, instead of being my usual, dire self, I'm actually happy.
And it's really embarrassing.

313.

I haven't met my soul mate yet.
Long-distance relationships are difficult.

314.

Hope is kind of like birds. In that I don't have any.

315.

Luckily, not only is it easy to die, it's also easy for people
to forget you once you're dead.

316.

God loved me. It was great at the time, but now I feel used.

317.

Life is defined by temporality. Like rainbows.

318.

Sunsets are pretty until you stop looking at them.

319.

Sometimes after a really good sunset, I feel like a pumped-up,
on-top-of-the-world version of myself, and I realize that
I'm better than everybody else. Compared to how great I am,
everybody else is basically meaningless. Then I remember
how I will die in obscurity.

320.

I am dramatically affected by changes in the light.
It might be because I'm a vampire.

321.

Today is just crazy.

322.

You shouldn't have blown out that candle. Now it's harder to see,
and some people might trip over something and die.
You should feel really, really bad right now about all those
people who you just basically killed.

323.

All of my role models are imaginary. In this way I can aspire to
goals that are unreachable and by being constantly disappointed in
myself I can be all the more ensconced in the lives of my imaginary
friends to the point where I no longer exist and in that way begin
to approach the sacral plane on which they exist or, rather, do not.

324.

No one cares about me. Maybe if I was good at something
people would care about me. Or maybe if I killed my daughter and
led an army to war and then got home only to be murdered by
my adulterous wife people would care about or at least notice me.

325.

This one day I had sex all day. That day, words were as useful to
me as clothes are to Jesus. Which is to say: useless.

326.

Heaven is so 1861.

327.

Every painter fails against the task of rendering the world and
its beauty. What they just don't get for some reason is that beauty
is made up of flamingoes. Gold flamingoes, with sapphires
for eyes, which are on fire.

328.

Naked people always win in a fight.

329.

Sometimes when I'm feeling really intense I don't really feel
anything. It is at these times when I want to open my body up like
a sexual door. Knock on me already, Sue.

330.

God's into bondage. I'm only kind of into bondage,
but I'm getting used to it.

331.

This one time I saw a ghost. It wasn't really a big deal.
He was kind of shy. For some reason he was wearing a lace dress.
He looked okay in it.

332.

You're better than me. You're also better than God. I want you
to filter me down until you find something good in this pile of
Emily Dickinson and take it with you as a keepsake to remember
me by. Like one of my teeth or a kidney or something.

333.

I have only ever heard one thing. I cannot stop hearing it.
Everything repeats this one thing to me. There is a voice in the
landscape, saying this one thing to me. If you map out the bones
of my body when I'm asleep, they will spell out this one thing.
If you ask me to, I cannot tell you what this one thing is. I am a
little unbalanced. I should've mentioned that.

334.

I like aleatoric music.

335.

I like Sue's smile because it reminds me of when she isn't smiling.
How sad I am when she isn't smiling. How terrible the world
is almost constantly.

336.

Sight is intimately connected to ownership. And I am blind.

337.

Sometimes ghosts come back from the dead just to spend time with
me. Zombies too. And they bring all these things that I lost—like
my old watch or some socks or something. The ghosts say "Hi" to
the zombies. The zombies ask me what I've been up to these days.
"Nothing much," I say. And they nod. They feel sorry for me.

338.

God, I want you to tie me to a horse and set it running. Then I can
spend all my time moving forward, strapped to the back of a horse,
waving goodbye to things.

339.

One of my hobbies is watching people die. People seem very
honest when they're about to die. It's kind of refreshing. I'm sorry,
I guess that's a weird hobby.

340.

Suddenly it is as if all plurality became one thing, and in
becoming so died. Or else just I died.

341.

Calm down, the worst thing that could happen to you is death.

342.

I used to have a lot of imaginary friends. But they all disappeared.
I should've locked them up in cages and tortured them until
they answered my questions about the nature of their existence.

343.

I like to stand at the top of hills or tall buildings and look down
upon the world and feel better than it.

344.

Now that I'm dead, I can't wait until my friends and family die,
so we can all have zombie Thanksgiving together.

345.

Instead of being afraid of death, I fetishize it.
Because I'm a Christian.

346.

This guy wanted to have sex with me, and I kept turning him
down, so he killed himself. Now the zombie version of this guy
comes around and still wants to have sex with me. I don't know
how to turn him down. He obviously likes me. I might just do it.

347.

I hate change.

348.

I'm tired of being an artist. I would rather be the object
of all human praise.

349.

Having sex is kind of like dying.

350.

Dying is kind of like having sex.

351.

I saw this cat hunting a bird. Its eyes dilated and it wiggled its butt and then it pounced and the bird flew away. I'm sorry, cat.

352.

Eternity is both infinitely slow and fast.

353.

I no longer go by Emily Dickinson. You can call me Queen Emily Dickinson now.

354.

If somebody's friend just died, sometimes I like to rub it in by reminding them of how wonderful their friend was when he was alive, how he wore his hair, how he smiled in a way that always reminded you of something though you couldn't quite say what, how he invented inside jokes with you in the church, how you hid in the corner together at that boring party, and how he's dead to this world completely. Then they usually start to cry.

355.

My sadness is actually more intense than normal-people's sadnesses as it creates a cipher that cannot be translated into normal-people language.

356.

Dear sir. I miss you. Let me know if you're going to visit me so
I know whether I should kill myself or not.

357.

Sometimes I get confused when I look in a mirror. Who is that?

358.

Maybe I am greedy. I don't know. All that I want is *everything*.

359.

I saw this bird.

360.

Sometimes my soul hangs out of my body a little when
I'm around my brother's girlfriend.

361.

You're all going to burn in the fires of Hell if you don't start
believing in Jesus Christ our Lord and Savior.

362.

I like simple things. Like friendship. And sunshine. And flowers.
What else. Oh, I like hills. I guess that's about it.

363.

I know what happens in October. Autumn happens in October.

364.

I like concepts that are diametrically opposed to each other,
because they present a great distance between them in
which everything exists.

365.

Somewhere, it is probably possible to be happy.
What can I say, I'm optimistic.

366.

Jesus raped me.

367.

I displace my sexual urges by gardening. Flowers are yonic.

368.

I really like this guy. I want to be everything that comes into
physical contact with him. These things include: water, dust
particles, certain insects, his clothing, light, himself…

369.

Death makes people imaginary.

370.

Sometimes I see hummingbirds. I really like hummingbirds.

371.

Happiness is more important than shoes.

372.

If nothing else, you have to admit Death's got style.

373.

I am interested in the indeterminacy of language as this
indeterminacy extends beyond the realm of communication into
the very existence of objects, or rather, the hypothesized existence
of said objects. There is nothing greater at alerting the senses
to the possibility of a world both spiritual and narcotic than doubt.
Option, multiple, chance, sequel—these are the real factors
that bind us to every aesthetic experience, which is to say:
every experience.

374.

It will be summer. And then it will not be summer.

375.

I like things that aren't things at all. I guess I mean I don't like
things.

376.

I'm hunting down this little girl. I just found her little book.
And her little hat. Soon enough, I'm probably going to find her
little dead body.

377.

Apparently Jesus is too busy knocking down buildings, summoning
natural disasters at will, and just generally wreaking havoc to hang
out with me.

378.

I just heard this really catchy song. And now it's stuck in my head.
And now I'm pretty sure it'll be stuck in my head until I kill myself.

379.

I wish I were simpler. I also wish I were more edible.

380.

Your lips are so beautiful when they are moving.
Were you saying something, Sue? Kiss me.

381.

Sometimes I fantasize about being a ballerina.
Also, sometimes I fantasize about having claws for hands.

382.

I just got dumped. Do you want to be my rebound?

383.

I like trains. I like trains because they embody a sense of freedom
that seems innate in the very thrust of modernity.
Because they seem, unlike carriage horses, to be their sole owner.
And because they go: *choo, choo*.

384.

Murder makes a lot of sense when you think about it. Though
I guess it makes less sense after you've gone ahead and done it.

385.

I'm a little clingy. Can I make a necklace out of
some of your teeth?

386.

You should see God when he's all cleaned up.
He can be very handsome.

387.

The gravitational force of the moon on the Earth's oceans stretches them into an ellipse with the Earth in the center. This effect takes the form of two bulges—one nearest the moon and one farthest from it. Since these two bulges rotate around the Earth once a day as it spins on its axis, the oceans' water is continuously rushing toward them. And this is sexual.

388.

Now that my life has become devastated to the point where everything seems meaningless, I can be happy again, because I only have this long drawn-out pain to deal with as opposed to that earlier, more extreme pain. Oh wait, no I can't.

389.

When I'm dead, people will be nicer to me. They might even remember my name: Saint Emily Dickinson.

390.

I don't think I'll just hang out in my grave when I'm dead. Instead I'll probably get restless and walk the Earth as a zombie.

391.

I wish I could forget things that I can't forget.
I would pay good money to forget certain things.
Do you know where I can buy some drugs?

392.

When I was younger, I experimented with other girls, but they never took it seriously.

393.

Without you, Sue, I am nothing. Scratch that. Without you, I am some things but not enough things to make up a human being.

394.

The worst part about being dead is how people pity you.

395.

When I die, I'm going to trade in my old face for a really awesome new face. Maybe I'll trade it in for Queen Victoria's face. She has a good face.

396.

They overcharged me for this drink. Story of my life.

397.

I went to a funeral and there was this bird at the funeral who apparently knew the guy who died and wanted to offer his condolences. Nobody seemed to think it was weird that he was a bird and could talk about things like human tragedy and grief.

398.

I hate people who die when it's really beautiful outside.

399.

Sometimes I feel very alone.

400.

Russians have a thing for hemlock. Hemlock has a thing for Russians: i.e., death.

401.

I have found a state of being so thorough that all other human functions become supplementary to this ecstasy which cannot maintain itself and which makes no attempts to do so. In this state, things can get kind of intense.

402.

Although sound comes from an external source, the interpretation of sound takes place internally. When I think about this too much I start to feel a little crazy.

403.

It makes sense to want to die, but for some reason I don't want to.

404.

Jesus already has a patent out on crucifixion.

405.

Things could've gone well, but they didn't.

406.

Dead people usually sign up for band camp when they die. Then they usually play in a zombie marching band constantly for the rest of eternity.

407.

I have a gun, but I only use it when the voices tell me to.

408.

I like summer. Summer's great.
Speaking of summer, is it summer yet?

409.

If souls were people they would be assholes.

410.

I want to be inside of you. I mean if I were a boat and you were the ocean. I guess I mean in general. This is a long way of saying that I want to go sailing with you, Sue.

411.

Mine.

412.

She only looked a little bit dead but she was actually entirely dead.

413.

God forgot where he put Heaven. I think he put it inside of that crazy guy over there.

414.

Happy things are actually sad, sad things.

415.

This fat guy died. It took a lot more to kill him than other, smaller people.

416.

Sad children are sad.

417.

I don't really know what money is. Because I'm an alien.

418.

I am attracted to you, because you are rich.

419.

Everyone dies. That means you, toad. That also means you, king of the toads.

420.

Right when you least expect it: menopause.

421.

I feel better about past events that made me feel really bad at the time. I think it's because I'm a little older now and can understand those earlier situations and place them in a larger context.

422.

When people are buried alive, by an avalanche or something, they quit whining.

423.

My brain thinks it's funny that I'm crazy.

424.

Without markers, it would be hard to tell where we hid all those dead bodies.

425.

Always expect the worst, and it will arrive on time.

426.

I'm friends with this guy. There are many benefits to having him as a friend. One of them is sex.

427.

Eclipses are kind of weird if you aren't familiar with the astronomical principles that govern them.

428.

In dim light or darkness, the human eye adapts by widening its pupil to let in as much light as possible. This slow adjustment to the dark is not unlike how you gradually get used to being a vampire.

429.

Where's God, you say? Right up ahead and to the left. Trust me, you can't miss Him. (He's the omnipotent-looking naked guy made of a celestial fire sitting next to Jesus.)

430.

Sometimes it feels good to lie to yourself.

431.

I can't wait for you to die so I can make love to your dead body. I hope you don't mind, Sue.

432.

I cannot write people back to life. As hard as I might try. And I do. Furiously. Like a wizard. Or a grammarian.

433.

I promised some leprechauns not to tell you that I saw them.

434.

I think most dead things are happy.

435.

I don't really want to know things.

436.

The sun is why we can see the sun.

437.

I would avoid God and religion completely if it weren't for that one small thing: eternal punishment.

438.

Bodies are kind of like birdhouses. Take that person for example. Oh wait, that's a birdhouse.

439.

Everyone likes a buffet. Unless you're anorexic.

440.

I visited my childhood home the other day and thought about knocking on the door, but then I got scared and ran away.

441.

The more people die, the easier it gets for you to do it. Because you get depressed. Because everyone is dead. And then you want to die. And then you do.

442.

I can see you better when it's dark and therefore harder to see, because you don't exist.

443.

If you weren't human, I could probably relate to you better.

444.

I'm hungry!

445.

My parents used to lock me in a closet when I was annoying them. I think that's called child abuse.

446.

Poets can make dead things smell really good.

447.

A bunch of trees fell on this one lumberjack. All the other lumberjacks tried to save him. But he died and went to lumberjack heaven—where the trees fell themselves, where the rivers fill with logs, and where plaid lines the fields from one horizon to the next.

448.

Now that I'm a zombie, I have sleepovers all the time.

449.

I'm an early-morning person. Every other time of day sucks.

450.

It's what's on the inside that counts. Except sometimes it isn't.

451.

I don't know how to swim, but I wanted to get some pearls, so I got some poor people to get them for me.

452.

It's hard to have sex all by yourself.

453.

What should we do now that we're dead? I guess we could give God a call and have him show us around.

454.

I was dating this guy when he got a fatal illness. I thought it would bum me out, but it was actually really fun to be in that position of mourning and to watch him slowly die and to sing all those sad songs and to go to his funeral looking great.

455.

I'm rich. And proud of it. But instead of punitory accumulation, I'm referring to spiritual wealth.

456.

I'm finally getting used to the societal constraints that are forced on me by the larger populace. The rules do not seem arbitrary inasmuch as they purposefully demoralize our innate human freedom that follows an urge deeper than the majority's desire for general consensus and order. Maybe when I'm dead I can be a little more human than these standards require us to be, at these dinner parties, attended by my fellow prisoners of decency.

I mean I want to bite somebody.

457.

Trees live longer and better than people do. Damn it.

I want to be a tree.

458.

Robots are mean because they don't understand human emotions.

459.

I don't know why I love you, Sue.

I think maybe I love you because things exist.

460.

Yetis like flowers.

461.

Now that you're dead I want you to know that
I always liked your face.

462.

Life is kind of like a bird. More specifically: a bobolink.

463.

That person is asleep. Oh, actually, that person
is starting to decompose.

464.

I wouldn't want things if I were dead.

465.

In some ways, the Battle of Antietam shares a beauty similar
to that of autumn. They both involve death spreading over an
increasingly red landscape.

466.

I'm homeless. Anything can happen when you're homeless!

467.

I like how God is watching us, eager to kill each one
of us when the time's right.

468.

I am horrified by sunsets.

469.

I'm kind of like a little pearl in the ocean of life.

470.

I still remember that time when you were really encouraging.
Thank you for encouraging me that one time when I was down.

471.

Zombies don't have a good sense of personal hygiene.

472.

Stop being so sad. Your troubles are meaningless.

473.

I'm a stereotype of myself.

474.

If you really loved God, you'd kill yourself so
you could go see him.

475.

I am a lonely carpenter. Sometimes I talk to myself.
Sometimes I also talk to my hammer.

476.

Death isn't a place so much as it is a state in which Heaven can't
logically exist as a real thing but rather as an idea placed on an idea
by those who are still alive and therefore still able to be irrational.

477.

Have I mentioned that sex is linked inexorably to death, Sue?

478.

God is kind of like a genie who doesn't listen to you.

479.

I went on a date with this guy, and it was nice but in a boring kind
of way. Then it was getting late and I was getting cold because
I was wearing this really skimpy dress, but luckily we finally got to
his place. It wasn't so much a place as it was the underworld,
but it's not like I could say, hey, hold on, buddy.
I was already dead. Whatever.

480.

People who want to die are less likely to die. I don't know the
difference between irony and justice.

481.

I'm famous to myself.

482.

General James Wolfe died happy because he died doing what
he loved the most: i.e., killing French people.

483.

I gave some food to a bird.

484.

Sometimes I'm a robot. Sometimes I'm a zombie. I guess
I'm a robot-zombie.

485.

Death is mean.

486.

I kidnapped a homeless person.

487.

You can know what time it is based on signs in the
natural world such as the heightening shadows of a tree
or of a house cast on the lawn.

488.

You think you are very important. I think you are very important,
and I love you.

489.

My faith in God is something that has physical properties
which you can calculate using a standard system of measurement.
And it's really big.

490.

Some people are nocturnal. Vampires, for example.

491.

Dying people love me.

492.

I like to help people because it makes me feel better than them.

493.

I get cold when I'm sad. I need a sweater.

494.

You can find out a lot about people by smelling them.

DICKINSON, CONTEMPLATING THE INEVITABILITY OF DEATH.

495.

Today is a beautiful naked old lady.

496.

Poor children have a higher mortality rate because they are
God's favorite people to kill.

497.

One plus one is one.

498.

I live in constant fear. At least it distracts me from my constant state
of depression.

499.

The only way to experience pleasure is by comparison.

500.

I'm watching you… waiting.

501.

The robin is a species of birds that is most visibly present in
spring and that makes its nest inside trees. It is a species that hates
surprises. It also dislikes sinners.

502.

Everybody is dying. Everything is death. (Which is great!)

503.

When my friend dies, I'm not going to tell anyone. That way
she'll still be legally alive. And no one will bury her. And I can go
see her whenever I like, because she'll always stay right where
I left her dead body.

504.

I experience the world as a simultaneous system in which
it is difficult to distinguish one event from another and thus hard
to determine the causality of its parts. Birds make the sun rise
by singing at it.

505.

These flowers smell like a metaphor for something.

506.

Light is a communist.

507.

God loves forest fires. He also likes to wear dresses.

508.

The existence of this world—and all the people that make it up—is
one big gaping hole in which we are all just waiting to die.

509.

There is a strangeness to the mutability of clouds which I find
attractive. I wish the president of the United States were a cloud.
I elect that cloud over there that looks like a moose, and now a
whale, and now a trumpet, to be president of the United States.

510.

You can't buy souls in Switzerland. In America, you can buy souls
(and for cheap).

511.

I love you, cowboy Jesus, even though you branded me, and then
left me, and I never see you anymore.

512.

I really like to read.

513.

Art is destroyed by the blind utility of the masses.

514.

I never saw the ocean so beautiful as when I drowned.

515.

I like extreme pain because it distracts me from the dull,
constant pain of living.

516.

Heaven does not obey the law of gravity or other scientific
principles. It either operates on a higher mathematical order than
logic or, more likely, on a lower one.

517.

Every life simultaneously composes the entire
world and almost nothing of it.

518.

Angels like to watch people die.
I want Sue to want to watch me.

519.

Both the problem with and the genesis of my seemingly
limitless passion is the one-sided nature of myself and
everything that makes me up.

520.

Gentians bloom in the winter instead of the spring. I like them
because they're "different," like me.

521.

It wasn't very nice for God to forbid Moses from going into the
Promised Land after all that work. I'm just saying.

522.

I do all my little, useless tasks because otherwise
I wouldn't have any.

523.

I saw a painting that made things look better than they look.

524.

I prefer zombies to living people. They have a stronger sense
of moral justice and a better sense of style.

525.

God is homeless. And a little mangy.

526.

I don't have any money. Maybe we can arrange something.
I can offer you either flowers or sex.

527.

What seems like the end of the entire world is really just the end
of your small, unimportant one.

528.

Some people go to Florida in the winter. I don't
go to Florida, on principle.

529.

I am a bad zookeeper.

530.

Jesus was really good at delivering a memorable public image.

531.

I'm totally retarded for you.

532.

I suffer from seasonal depression. Cows also suffer
from seasonal depression.

533.

Poets are more important than all existence.

534.

How many people do you think are masturbating right now who
would rather be having sex with each other? Probably a lot.

535.

If I weren't so sad, I might not feel as lonely as I do.
Then again, maybe it's even lonelier being happy.

536.

There's a difference between being rich and being loaded.
One involves money and the other involves Divine Power.

537.

I want to know what death is like so much I could die.

538.

Sadness makes everything beautiful. Like Jesus, during his crucifixion. He never looked so pretty.

539.

Pleasure doesn't belong to us. It's Sue's.

540.

Just do it.

541.

Forgive me for not killing myself on your behalf.

542.

I am in love with the world's largest woman.
She has a big body, and all her organs are big too.

543.

Zombies are really awkward at tea parties and other social settings.

544.

I can kind of guess what Heaven will look like. Pretty little clouds, birds, really good lighting. But what I really want to know is how beautiful I'll be when I'm an angel.

545.

God's really good at remembering faces.

546.

I used to pray, but then I realized how annoying it would be to have someone asking things from you all the time, and I didn't want to risk facing the wrath of God. Either way, even going through the motions is a hassle, since I inevitably feel empty afterward, because God is a social construct.

547.

One of my neighbors died. I think I'll sit here and watch his family suffer from a distance.

548.

Blackberries are better than Jesus because they don't complain when you eat them.

549.

The moon exists.

550.

My pain is more painful than everyone else's pain ever. Except maybe Jesus's.

551.

Sometimes when I'm cold I pretend that I'm not cold to comfort myself.

552.

Depression sucks.

553.

I used to work for a butterfly. But then I got fired.

554.

Everything between us—every article of clothing, every hair,
every layer of skin—is like a prison wall through which I
will burrow to get to you, Sue, despite the fact that there are also
dragons hiding in that wall which I will have to fend off to be
close enough to you that we can finally fuse our bodies together
and become one being.

555.

We should sneak into that abandoned house over there.
I think there's a dead body in it.

556.

Death is really awkward and has a bad sense of interior decoration.

557.

Words represent things even when they don't.

558.

There's this rockperson who keeps running around killing things.

559.

All the dirty and perhaps sordid means necessary to produce sexual
fulfillment are justified by the sublimity of release.

560.

After having an orgasm, I always feel a little empty inside.

561.

The greatest human discoveries were made by people
who proceeded through life in an illogical manner
and then got really lucky.

562.

Hit me. I love you.

563.

Brains do whatever they want. Sometimes brains want to go crazy.

564.

The day is the last part of the day to happen before it stops.

565.

Happiness cannot be destroyed, but it can be lost,
forgotten, buried, etc.

566.

My friend Carmine has a beautiful green face.

567.

Is it God's fault you're unhappy? Probably yes.

568.

$e = mc^2$

569.

I love books. So much. I want to have sex with them.

570.

I tried to think of what the saddest thing in the world was so
long that I became it.

571.

Sometimes I don't know if I'm talking about butterflies or people
because of the mutable nature of language.

572.

Have I mentioned that I like sunsets? I like all kinds of sunsets. Also, Jewish people are shiny.

573.

This guy gave me a really sexy look, and then I gave him a really sexy look, and then we both felt really sexy.

574.

I only like approximately two people. I can't even name all the countless numbers of people who I'd prefer dead.

575.

I'm always prepared to be made Queen of the Universe just in case someone comes up to me out of nowhere and asks me to be Queen of the Universe.

576.

Instead of worrying, I prefer to despair.

577.

Heaven is a small, boring suburb kind of like Amherst, except covered in feathers.

578.

How to spend a typical day in the life of Emily Dickinson:
1. Lie around.
2. Look out the window.
3. Compare things to Sue.
4. Die a little inside.

579.

Sometimes I own myself, and sometimes myself owns me.

580.

One person's fulfillment is another person's sad, sad existence.

581.

God doesn't care about me. He thinks I'm greedy. All I really want from him is to never have been born.

582.

Dead people hate summer. Everyone's too busy having parties and sex to pay them any attention. I'm sorry, dead people.

583.

I am a natural disaster.

584.

Sometimes I like to pretend that I'm dead. Ah, that feels nice.

585.

My brain wants out of my body and is slowly planning its escape.

586.

I'm not good at social interactions. Instead of saying "good morning" or "hello" or some other such salutation, I always say "goodnight," no matter what time it is. Because I'm dark like that.

587.

Some girls have all the luck. Dead girls, for example.

588.

Hearts are really needy organs. Mine needs
my brother's girlfriend.

589.

Sometimes everything is made of opals. I love opals.

590.

Most people would rather masturbate than read a book.

591.

Hearing is the last thing to leave the body and is thus perhaps
the most horrifying of the senses.

592.

God came to visit me and won't leave, and now I can't leave,
out of common courtesy, so I guess I'll just stay in my room with
Him and slowly grow crazier until I die.

593.

Unfortunately, I can't follow the moon because
I would have to travel about four-thousand miles per hour
to match the Earth's rotational speed.

594.

Hope is worse than doom.

595.

Thunder is louder than lightning.

596.

I was in love with a woman, so we got married,
but now she's dead.

597.

This emperor keeps throwing rubies at me.
Ow, stop throwing rubies at me.

598.

God is a nice thought.

599.

I don't play in graveyards very much because, inconveniently,
they are chock-full of sad people.

600.

I love Elizabeth Barrett Browning. She is a really good poet. I want
to have sex with her. I want to marry Elizabeth Barrett Browning
and take her virginity in our honeymoon suite somewhere in Italy.

601.

The meaning of life cannot exist before the life whose meaning
is in question doesn't.

602.

Certain deaths are fashionable. I heard death by childbirth
is really in this season.

603.

The sun wants to destroy the sky, but it can't.

604.

You know who I'm talking about. She's the one
who always wears velvet and that orange vest and instead
of feet she has hands. She's kind of intense.

605.

I am alive but only because I'm not dead. On another note,
sometimes I want you to give birth to me.

606.

It's always summer when you're a nymph.

607.

I hate having to wait for a cab.

608.

I don't know which I like more: happiness or sadness. I guess
probably happiness. No, now I'm just lying to myself.

609.

It is hard to distinguish night from day at the moment
of their intersection.

610.

Butterflies are really full of themselves. They like to fly around,
looking good, pitying everyone.

611.

I fell in love with my imaginary friend. And then she died. Or else I
stopped imagining her. Or else she stopped imagining me?

612.

Opposites attract. That's why I'm attracted to inexistence.

613.

It was just an ordinary day until I suddenly apotheosized.

614.

Dead people don't generate heat.

615.

God likes to watch.

616.

You can't kill me if I'm already dead.

617.

I enjoy sitting on you, couch. Especially when it's cold outside.

618.

You love me. You love me not. You will probably never love me, ever, for the rest of eternity.

619.

Are you still a virgin?

620.

Logic is a trap from which only crazy people can escape.

621.

The wind came to visit me, so I let him in, but because he isn't familiar with the standard courtesies of a houseguest, and because he isn't comprised of solid matter. It was kind of awkward.

622.

The sun is awesome. And sneaky.

623.

Humans may only talk to God through a long tube connected to his ear.

624.

Dead people don't really care about anything.
Because they're dead.

625.

I won't cheat on you, like those other tramps.

626.

Imaginary food tastes better than food.

627.

I went crazy but it was a good kind of crazy.

628.

Trinkets turn me on.

629.

I am a civil war. Sue is the new union I want to
establish as an independent nation.

630.

Souls enjoy space travel.

631.

I am going to drown myself to prove how much I love you.
You're welcome.

632.

It's better to be homeless than to lack a system of belief.

633.

This one time I touched the universe, and it exploded, and then
no one existed except me. I'm sorry about that.

634.

I guess I'm pessimistic.

635.

I wish I were rich so I could waste my money on a slut like you.

636.

At every moment, I am being struck by lightning.

637.

Someone please wake up that dead person so I can thank her
for being so nice to me.

638.

The future does what it wants.

639.

Happiness requires hard work and a desperate sense of ownership.

640.

The death of an artist makes his or her work increase in value
because of the public's fascination with its own mortality.
Its willingness to view the art in question outside of previous
negative political connotations that might have arisen from
the artist's counternormative lifestyle stems partially from the
particular work and partially from the particular artist but mostly
from the subjects of mourning and their need to cope with
a refreshed awareness of their own death and death's consequences.
By collectively celebrating the deceased and his or her creative
act, they are protecting the general idea of legacy, thereby
protecting their own.

641.

Shh, don't let people know that it is possible for me not to exist.

642.

The most beautiful person in the world is so stupid and full of
herself that she doesn't even know she's dead. And so beautiful
that everyone wants to have sex with her anyway.

643.

It's best to keep secrets. Especially if they're secrets
about horrifyingly abhorrent crimes against humanity that
you have committed.

644.

The life-death exchange rate is better here than in the realms
of the afterworld, so you should probably trade in your currency
before you go.

645.

It's easier to become intoxicated by religious feeling than
by alcohol. I should know, since I'm a violent,
lustful, and constant drunk.

646.

If you don't learn math you will grow up to be a homeless person.

647.

To fill a hole, you have to fill it all the way.

648.

I watched this person die, and right before he died he kept looking
around for something, and I have no idea what he was looking for.

649.

I have another body inside of my body that is invincible against sharp objects.

650.

God likes it when people are friends with each other. And when they're more than friends, Sue.

651.

Your success makes other people feel sorry for themselves.

652.

All you need is love and dead Jesus on a cross.

653.

Against the apparent perpetuity of space and time, I cannot reasonably assert my individuality.

654.

If you try to catch beauty, God will kill you.

655.

Butterflies do things. Or sometimes they don't.

656.

I had a really good time at the beach.
I brought my dog, Carlo. We saw some mermaids and some warships. And then the sea had sex with me.

657.

Don't cry for dead people. I hate dead people.

DICKINSON, SIMULTANEOUSLY AROUSED AND DISGUSTED
BY THE THOUGHT OF SEX.

658.

Just because people weren't nice to me doesn't mean they should automatically go to hell. They should only maybe go to hell.

659.

The older, more experienced zombies should take the new, up-and-coming zombies out and show them the ropes.

660.

I accidentally hit myself in the face.

661.

Sometimes things can only be seen sometimes.

662.

One time I woke up before everyone else did and I went outside half naked, and it felt good.

663.

I am afraid of people who don't talk very much, because I assume they are smarter than me and are just sitting there, quietly judging me.

664.

Dead people who have been stabbed to death like to walk around with the knife still stuck in them in order to show off.

665.

The artist's work is more important than the artist.

666.

I went on a road trip last weekend. In my mind.

667.

The year is made up of months.

668.

All the best things are a little shameful.

669.

Even humanity is attractive at sunset.

670.

Get over yourself, Jesus. People get crucified all the time.

671.

Everyone should have sex. Virgins are traitors to the human race.

672.

Death came by, but you weren't here. He said to drop by
his place sometime when you get the chance.

673.

Postage rates are getting out of control.

674.

My feet keep telling me what to do. I am constantly
buying new shoes.

675.

Housewives are a boring and hideous breed of people.

676.

The moon kind of looks like your face.
I guess that's a compliment.

677.

If the nineteenth century were a person, he would be profoundly and irrevocably disturbed by all of the horrible things that he bore witness to and now has to keep secret for the sake of any remaining human decency.

678.

Sometimes I forget about the divine firmament and its endless glory, because I get distracted by candy.

679.

Note to self: nighttime ends at sunrise, at which point you should get dressed.

680.

I'm a paparazzo for God.

681.

I'm so good at sewing I can do it in my sleep, or when I'm dead. In fact, I'll probably be the best zombie seamstress ever.

682.

I love Sue more than Jesus loves Christians.

683.

Your soul is antsy for you to die.

684.

Happiness doesn't like death.

685.

No one asked you anything, ocean. Shut up. And, while you're at it, stop killing my friends.

686.

Nature doesn't care about Jesus. And that makes Jesus sad.

687.

Brazil is mad that I don't really want to go to Brazil.

688.

I really want to know what my friend was thinking when he died,
but I don't know how to ask him.

689.

Dead people love Heaven because they don't have a choice.

690.

The future does not exist until it is the present at which point
it is not the future anymore.

691.

When married people die they get married again in Heaven,
the only difference being that then they are both babies and
are both married to a baby, which is kind of weird.

692.

God is sensitive to people's problems.

693.

I'm in an abusive relationship with myself.

694.

For every silver lining, there's a cloud.

695.

I cannot access what I need to survive, and I like it that way.

696.

The only way this sunset could be any better is if I were dead.

697.

I'm a very anxious person.

698.

I'm living with this guy even though we aren't married, like Sue and my brother. His name is "Death." I don't know. It's alright.

699.

I'm cheating on you because you are a small, insignificant person compared to the other person I've been seeing.

700.

My favorite way to interact with people is to read letters from them, completely alone, in a locked room.

701.

Children are better than real people.

702.

I wouldn't be so sad if I weren't Emily Dickinson.

703.

The sun came up this morning, and I saw it.

704.

Today sucks balls.

705.

Although it's kind of embarrassing to be an old maid, I'm glad I never got married to a human.

706.

I cannot be with you because you would make me happy,
and that's not my style.

707.

Obese people hate small things.

708.

I'm obsessed with your face. I want my face to be welded
to your face forever.

709.

I have suicidal tendencies.

710.

Humans can't survive inside of the sun because it is in
a constant state of combustion, which keeps it at a temperature
of approximately five million degrees Celsius.

711.

God tried to kill me.

712.

I asked this guy to marry me, and it scared him off.

713.

Thanks so much for the endless amount of pain you gave me.
Really. I'm not being sarcastic. Thanks.

714.

Angels are plotting to destroy you.

715.

Dying is really trippy.

716.

Just when you need it the least, you find a pearl. I told you to get away from me, pearl. Shoo.

717.

The stars promised me they would last forever, but they lied. All stars will inevitably die as their potential energy is limited by their finite mass. I'm going to sue them.

718.

I have a vestigial third ear that I keep hidden because it's kind of embarrassing.

719.

Because you died, I have turned into a long, narrow excavation in the ground, the earth from which is thrown up in front to serve as a shelter from enemy fire or attack.

720.

What if there were a sea inside the sea that was inside the sea that was inside the sea that was inside the sea… that was inside the sea?

721.

We cannot create a philosophy of abstract thought unless it is born out of the materiality of the concrete world.

722.

Pallbearers are always the coolest people at a funeral.

723.

Does anyone else have seasonal depression? If so, please raise your hand.

724.

Everyone wants something even if they don't want anything.

725.

I don't know.

726.

I'm poor, so I have to give all my girlfriends fake diamonds instead of real diamonds.

727.

Have you heard of this great new product? Jesus swears by it. It's called Death™.

728.

St. Peter is kind of like an owl.

729.

I don't need my body anymore.

730.

I love balloons.

731.

I just had some major déjà vu.

732.

I don't know where my religion ends and my sex begins.

733.

I prefer the kind of happiness you can touch. Named Sue.

734.

You're going to be sorry for being such a jerk
to me when I'm famous and so rich that I can wear a belt
made entirely of live eagles.

735.

I mean, sure, the moon is pretty, but she's a little too fat for me.

736.

I'm willing to surgically alter my body in any way possible if it will
please you. Like if you want me to get a horn implanted onto my
forehead, just say the word.

737.

It's hard to prove that the world is not a horrible place that
is almost constantly ravaged by war and other human atrocities.

738.

The inevitability of death kind of puts a damper on everything.

739.

I need some new eyeballs, because mine have gone out of fashion.

740.

God is kind of like the FDIC.

741.

Mother Nature has her work cut out for her, since all her
children keep trying to eat each other.

742.

You can imprison people, but you can't prevent them from deluding themselves into thinking they're not in prison.

743.

Miracles are awesome. I'm made up mostly of miracles.

744.

I'm a necrophiliac.

745.

Mountains, you are my best friend.

746.

The ocean doesn't care that it killed my friends.

747.

God's into role-playing.

748.

Poor people are consistently better than rich people.

749.

I want to live inside of you like a parasite, Sue.

750.

I'm going to go on an antiwater diet.

751.

I still really like you even though you're a slut.

752.

Have you been to Mt. Teneriffe? It's in Washington. It's a really nice mountain.

753.

When I am sad, I feel like a fat, tongueless mouse-thief who
is also good at juggling.

754.

Sometimes I like to pretend to be a schoolgirl.
Will you be my schoolmaster?

755.

I will mold to fit your body.

756.

I only care about other people's deaths because they remind
me of my own mortality.

757.

I think somewhere there are people who have the
ability to be happy.

758.

I wish I could shrink myself down and go inside of a flower.
That would be great.

759.

Zombies have the best weddings.

760.

And on the first day, God created pain and suffering.

761.

Instead of using a bank, I prefer to avoid the capitalistic regime
by keeping all my possessions in birds' nests.

762.

Promise me that you'll call me right before you die, so I can be the one to close your eyes, with my mouth.

763.

I'm too lazy to hate people.

764.

See *My Emily Dickinson*, by Susan Howe (pp. 76–120).

765.

The Earth is round and therefore sunrises and sunsets occur.

766.

Bobolinks don't care if you cut down their tree.
They're like, "Whatever."

767.

I'm really into obsession.

768.

The sun has a crush on the mountains. The mountains aren't that into it.

769.

This dead person used to be a person!

770.

My favorite thing to do is sit and think weird things to myself.

771.

Zombies have really good eyesight.

772.

The more I'm tortured, the more poetry I write. About Sue.

773.

There's an invisible person who follows me around all the time.
It's somewhat bothersome.

774.

Zombie scientists don't often publish their research.

775.

I don't mind surprises, but I hate suspense.

776.

Theatre is the most disturbing of the arts because it is made
up of living people.

777.

Life is accidental.

778.

I don't know why trees exist.

779.

Sight is a process of ownership.

780.

I get along better with dead people.

781.

Memory is the source of all sadness.

782.

A thing cannot be said to not exist, because in saying such, the thing that supposedly does not exist is addressed as a thing and therefore a thing that exists.

783.

Poltergeists aren't very friendly.

784.

Sometimes I feel really crazy. Mostly when I suddenly get dizzy and my body starts to neigh like a horse.

785.

I put some plates on a shelf, but the shelf wasn't sturdy, so they fell off and broke.

786.

Autumn's a show-off.

787.

Sometimes I confuse things with other things.

788.

All published poets are whores.

789.

Unfortunately, death is permanent.

790.

People are born small and slowly increase in size.

791.

I'm afraid I might get dumped because my boyfriend is more attractive than me.

792.

Even if people never see it, your face still exists.

793.

I hate it when my soul's mad at me.

794.

My friend has been dead for a year, and now she can't see anything, because she's dead.

795.

When God dies, my notion of truth will be altered.

796.

There was a big storm that knocked down a tree in my front yard, but my house wasn't damaged.

797.

Nature doesn't think scientifically. Like my illicit relationship with Sue.

798.

Although stars appear from certain vantage points to be smaller than the Earth, they are consistently larger in mass.

800.

God owes me a lot, but I know he's good for it.

801.

I believe in fairies. Though they only come out
during fairy season.

802.

I have an errand to run: I have to go light myself on fire.

803.

I have to find out about myself by myself.

804.

I enjoy tending to my grave, because then I know that I'll be buried
in the prettiest grave of them all.

805.

I have connections in Heaven.

806.

Instead of buying a house, my plan for retirement is to shrink
myself down so I can live inside a flower.

807.

I like to be in a foreign country because of the way it feels to be
in a foreign country.

808.

I am embarrassed that I am not a bee.

809.

My favorite people are people who almost died but then didn't.

810.

Most birds' songs are about sex.

811.

Winter resents being compared to summer.

812.

The sun is the sun.

813.

I wish I never knew that bitch.

814.

Conquistadors are really angsty.

815.

Zombies are sad because they don't fit in anywhere.

816.

Sometimes I like being dehydrated.

817.

When I die, I'm going to be a dog, endlessly chasing my tail.

818.

Mary gave birth to Jesus who is God who is her father who she
had sex with in order to give birth to Jesus. I think that makes her
her own grandmother.

819.

I'm not anorexic, I just prefer to eat abstract things like the idea
of food instead of actual food.

820.

I don't read newspapers because they get in the way
of my imagination.

821.

I wish you were sick so I could take care of you.

822.

My friend died during corn season, so now I associate it with him. I really enjoy eating corn.

823.

Being born feels really great. Death feels just okay.

824.

Affliction permeates everything. Even suburbs, believe it or not.

825.

Jesus just flew in from Heaven and boy are his arms tired.

826.

It's hard to be both smart and not an atheist.

827.

When I like someone, I like them all the way.

828.

I need need.

829.

I try to connect with other human beings by uprooting plants of the flowering variety and delivering them to the targeted person in the hopes of sparking a collegial social interaction.

830.

The best time to get to know someone is when they've just died.

831.

Vowing to love someone "till death do us part" is pathetic.
Zombie marriages are stronger and longer lasting than regular
people marriages.

832.

What are your plans for today besides killing yourself?
Do you want to get lunch?

833.

Pain distracts you from silly things like the past and the future,
so you can live life to the fullest.

834.

I'm worried that God's going to be mad at me for not being a
baby anymore when I die.

835.

You don't have to make sense if you truly believe in yourself.

836.

Death isn't racist.

837.

The sun and the moon are in a sadomasochistic relationship.

838.

I might be dead, but at least I have great hair.

839.

She might appear to be dead, but she's actually just on vacation.

840.

True love is reserved for fetuses and zombies. And sister-in-laws.

841.

Yeah, I was struck by lightning. So what?

842.

I only smile on the inside.

843.

I didn't realize at the time that I was happiest that that was the
happiest I would ever be.

844.

It's hard to look good when you're being pummeled with rocks.

845.

It's hard to know what time it is when you're buried underground.

846.

When it rains, it rains.

847.

I had no idea she was about to die. Now I feel stupid.

848.

God's shy.

849.

I don't think that's a tree even though everyone says it's a tree.
I think it's the ocean, and that squirrel is a really good swimmer.

850.

I stole stuff from that butterfly, and he can't do anything about it.

851.

Even now that you're dead, you're still annoying. Gimme, gimme, gimme: that's what you sound like.

852.

I thought about helping this guy out, but he's an asshole, so I didn't.

853.

This bird really wanted to go into outer space, so she did, and then she exploded, sending a cloud of feathers into orbit around the Earth.

854.

Don't knock death until you try it.

855.

Oh, you're immortal? Big deal. I'm immortal twice.

856.

I may be poor, but at least I don't have any money.

857.

Marriage is a system of oppression that women are asked to perpetuate by giving into a false notion of male domination, thereby lowering themselves to the position of property. Please pass the salt, Sue.

858.

Though time is infinite, I can take comfort in the fact that Mondays aren't.

859.

Sometimes it's good to doubt that you are queen of the world.

860.

My friend sneaked away to become a zombie without telling me.

861.

Time generally makes things worse.

862.

I work really hard at things that, by all standards,
appear to be fruitless.

863.

Flowers are pretty but kind of stupid.

864.

You should diversify your assets. Except you, Sue.
Your assets are fine.

865.

I prefer a really intensely agonizing kind of foreplay to any
actual sex whatsoever.

866.

The universe has ADHD.

867.

I knew I was having a mental breakdown when abstract concepts
started to make noise.

868.

You can tell a person is about to die when they start glowing in the dark.

869.

I can see the things that I can't see by lying to myself.

870.

People are greedy. Everyone wants to be able to eat.

871.

If you want to buy everything that exists, you'll need a lot of money.

872.

It's hard to throw a banquet if you don't have any food.

873.

I like it when I can hear a bird but I can't see one.

874.

Please be my friend even when I fuck things up.

875.

Purple is a good color. Witches love purple.

876.

My superpower is the ability to exist.

877.

The scariest thing for a lonely person is the possibility of company.

878.

Bees like making honey.

879.

I wish I could be as cool as a zombie.

880.

Meaningless labor is awesome.

881.

My girlfriend would rather be dead than be my girlfriend.
Right, Sue?

882.

The truth is that trees have a lot of pent-up aggression.

883.

South Americans are more attractive than North Americans.

884.

Love is a time machine.

885.

Sometimes I enjoy being a bitch.

886.

It's easier to get time off to travel when you're a zombie.

887.

A lot of my creative energy comes out of my sexual frustration.

888.

If I were a flower I would want you to pick me, thereby killing me.
Then I would want you to pin my dead corpse on your lapel.

889.

Sad people are bad at manual labor.

890.

A coffin might seem small, but it's big enough for a party.
I know from experience.

891.

I'm not homeless. I'm outdoorsy.

892.

All my favorite celebrities are zombies.

893.

Nature knows she's in charge and isn't shy about it.

894.

You can't catch someone if they're dead.

895.

Canada Day is nothing compared to the Fourth of July.

896.

Zombies love purple even when it's out of fashion.

897.

Instead of merely dying, she exploded.

898.

I like to spend my time hanging out with friends that I don't have.

899.

The law holds people accountable for things they have
no control over.

900.

I rented one of my vital organs from the hospital and now
I have to give it back.

901.

The relationship between the soul and the body is tentative.

902.

The relationship between the body and the soul is tentative.

903.

Escapism is what makes life worth living.

904.

I like to believe that walking under ladders
is unlucky because approaching life with a consistent
sense of logic is too heartbreaking.

905.

By dissecting a bird you can locate its vocal cords.

906.

Even though we live in the same city, we're in a
long-distance relationship.

907.

I'm glad I'm dead, but I hope death isn't death.

908.

Worms can't wait to eat us.
Actually, they can wait.
And they are.

909.

If you wanted to have sex with a bee, I would dress up
in a bee costume, Sue.

910.

Once you find something, you'll probably lose it. And then go
on an epic exploration looking for a mythical blanket. And then
you'll probably not find the magic blanket. And then you'll
probably realize that your whole life is a sham.

911.

You know it's cold outside when people start dying
of overexposure.

912.

Things exist no matter where you go.

913.

Matter contains potential energy.

914.

I was lost, and then I saw a family living in a house. Everyone
appeared to be so comfortable and at home there that I felt even
worse about being lost. I tried to join them, but they closed the
door before I could get inside. I just wanted to live with them.
I don't know why they wouldn't let me live with them.

915.

It's autumn, and I don't know what to do.

916.

Who lives in this mushroom?

917.

Ghosts like to haunt familiar places. They're not that into travel.

918.

The fact that I'm alive and that other people
are alive is very disorienting.

919.

I want to be so famous it physically crushes me.

920.

I prefer scars to jewelry.

921.

I hope it snows so that all the zombie children can have
a snowball fight.

922.

I like sunlight unless I'm hungover.

923.

I have a small crush on the man who delivers ice to our house.
I hope he notices when I'm dead and feels a little sad about it.

924.

I better be immortal. Otherwise, I'll be really sad.

925.

I don't care if someone kills me as long as they're attractive.

926.

I walk funny.

927.

Dying's worse than not dying. Just so you know.

928.

Nature is only important if humans say it is.

929.

Would you still love me if I were a zombie? Would you give me a big sloppy kiss on my rotting flesh zombie mouth?

930.

Poets die. Poems, on the other hand, corrode slowly.

931.

If the oceans wanted to take over the world again, there's not much stopping them.

932.

If God didn't survive on a steady diet of human souls, he would probably kill all of us immediately.

933.

I guess maybe Heaven isn't a prison.

934.

My friends died and now I don't know where they are.
Maybe Vegas.

935.

I guess it's autumn now. Summer is a sneaky little bitch.

936.

I guess it's nighttime now. Daylight is a sneaky little bitch.

937.

You either become a man by going through puberty and
gradually aging into adulthood, or you can just skip all that
and go ahead and die.

938.

Death is a commie.

939.

The only good things that exist in life don't exist.

940.

How often do you have sex and where can I go in order
to watch you have it, Sue?

941.

This guy probably drowned himself. I wonder what it was like.
I wonder if he'd mind if I took his hat. Probably not.

942.

Now that you're my slave, you don't get two weeks' paid vacation.

943.

I'm really upset that my slave got away, because you can't
buy them anymore.

944.

Nature's kind of gaudy.

945.

If someone's trying to kill you, the best thing
to do is hide until they give up, and then give yourself away.
That way you're the one in control.

946.

Dying is only unfortunate if you have friends. Luckily, I don't have any. Take that, death.

947.

I put my money in a savings account, so it could earn interest.

948.

God lets it all hang out in spring.

949.

Death always ruins a party.

950.

It's been two years and the raspberry bushes I planted in the backyard haven't produced any fruit. Come on.

951.

If nobody loves you, you should probably just go ahead and die already. Thanks, Sue.

952.

It's nobler to die at sea than to go on a cruise.

953.

God likes it when people make castles, because he enjoys making ruins.

954.

If you want my V-card, you have to give me yours.

955.

I sing when I'm scared.

956.

Everyone's beautiful. It just takes a lot more effort to see the beauty in certain people who aren't as attractive as the people who are actually beautiful.

957.

People should be allowed to hate their jobs and not get shit about it.

958.

It's spring. There are daffodils. Someone is sexually reproducing at this very moment.

959.

My dead mother finds me embarrassing.

960.

My heart isn't good at long-range planning.

961.

Dying people are pretty laid-back.

962.

Society distracts me from my precious hallucinations.

963.

It's hard to control nature. Nature or human nature will eventually destroy us.

964.

Zombies get no respect.

965.

I can't find Heaven. I couldn't find it in Connecticut, so it must be in Maine, or else Canada. I hear that Hell is located somewhere in the Midwest.

966.

Death is good because it cheers up people who really wanted certain people dead and who can now move on with their lives, happily ever after.

967.

Two lovers are dying of cold. The first lover says to the second: I think this is it. We're goners. The second one replies: No big deal, now we get to go to Heaven. So they did. And their friends slowly joined them, one by one. (I'm not very good at telling jokes.)

968.

Fame is nice but is also limited by the short span of human existence. I'm sorry, famous people.

969.

God's kind of like an old aunt who wears a lot of rhinestones and hugs you a little too hard. It's difficult to get away from her. Sometimes I wish I could go to the beach and be by myself. But it doesn't really matter where you go, she'll follow you there, because she's creepy like that.

970.

Mountains are like really old fat people.

971.

Peace and God are great, but I don't actually believe
in any of that crap.

972.

You either get into heaven or you don't. It doesn't really matter
what you do. It's all politics.

973.

When I die and death tells me I have to stay dead, I'm going to be
like, "No thanks," and see what happens.

974.

This entire town was on fire, so I called the fire department,
and they told me it was just the sunset.

975.

Someone died and I'm sad about that. Based on how sad I am, he
was probably the most important person to ever have existed.

976.

I don't know where they put the month of May now that it's over.
Though they might've put it somewhere about eleven months
in the future.

977.

I wish I was good at something like climbing mountains
so I could feel like I was better than other people.

978.

You have to believe in things that don't exist, like yourself.

979.

Bees have a really good sense of style.

980.

Love is important because it encourages sexual reproduction
and a general resistance to the natural human urge for death.
Except if it's with Sue.

981.

The Virgin Mary has enough magic up her sleeves to cure cancer.
She's just a lazy witch.

982.

I want to help people so I can feel good. I'll start with myself.

983.

Hurry up. I want to have weird sex with you.

984.

I can't get any satisfaction, and I prefer it that way.

985.

When I lie down on the grass, the grass is probably screaming
silently to itself.

986.

I'll have sex with you unless you're scary.

987.

I wish I was as sexy and as dead as my ex-girlfriend.

988.

Death wanted to have sex, but everyone turned him down,
so he gave up trying. He's not looking so good these days.
He kind of let himself go.

989.

Sometimes I forget that air exists.

990.

Woodpeckers burrow holes into trees in order to eat insects that
live inside of them.

991.

Trying is more important than succeeding unless it isn't.

992.

I didn't see her for three weeks and then I found out she was dead. I
hate the nineteenth century.

993.

Dead famous people don't care when famous people die.

994.

This guy I know shot himself in the head.

995.

I don't care about things because I care about things that don't
exist.

996.

I've never lived so good as I have since I became a zombie.

997.

People who are in Heaven are generally happier than people
who go to Hell.

998.

Happiness is nice, but I still want to suffer at least a little bit.

999.

Spring isn't spring unless I'm getting laid.

1000.

God's made sure that true happiness isn't possible until you go all
the way to Heaven. A girl's got to keep her secrets.

1001.

I'm a zombie and I like looking at your face.

1002.

The sky is making a funny face.

1003.

I like music so much I want to punch through a window.

1004.

There's no such thing as silence.

1005.

I like you and you can't do anything about it, Sue.

1006.

Though he wasn't famous when he died, he became famous
because he died.

1007.

If you're lying to me, my life will have to be destroyed.

1008.

Bells don't move until someone pulls them, at which point
they make noise.

1009.

I started working as a personal assistant. It kind of sucks.

1010.

The third law of thermodynamics is a law and not a theory.

1011.

The strongest people are also the most delusional.

1012.

Atoms might not seem important because they are small, but
they're important.

1013.

I got stood up and now I'm so upset that I want to destroy the sun.

1014.

It's winter and the only way I can imagine spring is by
remembering spring.

1015.

Daylight came to town and woke everyone up by walking
right into their houses without their permission, because
he's got no class.

1016.

It's hard to believe in fairies when you're dead.

1017.

Souls are itching to get the hell out of their bodies.

1018.

Sometimes I don't like being homeless.

1019.

The queen died. That poor old lady.

1020.

It's always summer if you live on the equator. Unless the sun
explodes and destroys the Earth.

1021.

Knowledge is boring.

1022.

Blue jays are pretty good birds. I like blue jays.

1023.

I'm so generous that I'm willing to not kill myself for you.

1024.

I don't like winter. I think we should vote on a bill that
abolishes winter.

1025.

I'd trade places with a dead person any day. Though I guess maybe
that's a bad idea.

1026.

Hills and other topographical features of the landscape are not supposed to attend public school.

1027.

The whole Christian notion of the afterlife sounds a little shady to me.

1028.

Blind people are better at seeing things that don't exist.

1029.

Now that I'm miserable I know what it's like to be happy.

1030.

I like this pathetic, lonely flower because it reminds me of myself.

1031.

I met this talking baby named Trotwood. Is this your baby? Did you really name your baby Trotwood?

1032.

Most guardian angels are actually dragons.

1033.

I've got a shitty life but some really good karma.

1034.

I saw a bird and now I can't see it because it flew away.

1035.

I wouldn't buy the Earth even if I could afford it. It's pretty low quality.

1036.

I'm living off the grid.

1037.

Dying people don't need very much. All they need is a glass of water, maybe some flowers, and to hurry up and die already.

1038.

Flowers don't really look like flowers unless they're in bloom. Same goes for women.

1039.

I love you so much I want you to eat my organs. Forks and knives are in the top drawer, Sue.

1040.

The best part about me is that I'm your slave.

1041.

You call that a mountain? Oh, really? That's cute. Good job with that.

1042.

Right before spring, I always get nervous that nature will forget how to do it.

1043.

Shit happens, and it's hard to choose which shit.

1044.

Summer isn't summer without a little bit of revolution.

1045.

Until she died, I didn't notice that she was actually a hot, roughly spherical ball of gas that shines as a result of nuclear fusion reactions in the core.

1046.

I like seeing things. I like seeing things and then approaching them and then seeing them up close.

1047.

I prefer people when they're not at church.

1048.

All this great stuff maybe could've happened I think. But it didn't.

1049.

I like watching local news.

1050.

I'm afraid of getting too attached to my body, since it's kind of a flake.

1051.

I can't wait for indoor plumbing to be more widely available.

1052.

I just saw a UFO.

1053.

I don't have very much money. Which is nice. I gave each of my dollars a name. This one's named Janice.

DICKINSON, LOOKING AT SUE.

1054.

I have freckles. Do you like my freckles?

1055.

Midnight is more fun if you're nocturnal.

1056.

Bees hate the police.

1057.

Just once, God would like to meet someone who doesn't
know who he is.

1058.

It's rude to talk about water when someone's thirsty or has to pee.

1059.

I prefer one-night stands. But only when they don't end.
And they're with Sue.

1060.

Life is a very complicated door that opens out onto itself. I guess
it's not complicated. I guess it's just your basic revolving door.

1061.

Death is kind of like a really big vagina.

1062.

I like the silent type. That's why most of my friends are actually
inanimate objects.

1063.

In Heaven, they don't have lamps or the Sun or anything.
The only way to see anything is by the glow that emits from
God's naked body. It's kind of frustrating, because you can't
just stay up late reading in bed unless you smuggle in a candle or
something and God gets really mad if you do this. He feels like you
don't appreciate his giant glow-in-the-dark body and its ability to
light up most things in its proximity.

1064.

I'm not going to eat, because I don't want to ruin my appetite, since
I'm about to cannibalize one of my friends, and I want to be hungry
enough to eat all of him.

1065.

Nature's got style. She never wears the same thing more than once.

1066.

Death is kind of boring and repetitious.

1067.

I'm having a bad hair day.

1068.

I wish I could spend my spring break in the afterlife.

1069.

I'd rather go to bird-and-squirrel Heaven than people Heaven.

1070.

Dead people turn into reusable materials. The first law
of thermodynamics is gross.

1071.

Ugly people are usually bad people.

1072.

I can't find this thing I want to find because it doesn't exist.

1073.

The best thing to do with a flower is to stick your finger right into its nectary. Here, give me your hand, Sue.

1074.

I'm so glad that my friends are coming to visit that I'm going to lock them in my basement and never let them leave.

1075.

All zombies are hopeless romantics.

1076.

Souls are something that God secretes from his soul glands.

1077.

From now on, I'm going to make a point of memorizing the shape of every cloud I see.

1078.

Bees hate politicians.

1079.

Virgins love death.

1080.

I want to pretend that it's not winter, but whenever I go outside in my swimsuit, I get really cold.

1081.

I like people who give me peanuts.

1082.

I like it when famous people die.

1083.

Whenever I sing in church, people stare at me, because after I take communion, my mouth is usually covered in blood.

1084.

My friend didn't like this guy, so she tried to kill him. When that failed, she just gave up and had sex with him.

1085.

The sunrise is kind of like a stereotypical Asian man.

1086.

Nature's favorite color is yellow, but she only uses it for special occasions. Like sunsets and urine.

1087.

I brush my teeth a lot because I don't want dentures.

1088.

I'm having a stroke! And it feels kind of good.

1089.

Zombies aren't that different from normal people, except that their bodies are rotting a little bit.

1090.

Dust is mostly dead human skin, just floating around.

1091.

I like telling jokes to myself. Ha!

1092.

I love cemeteries! Cemeteries make me feel great!

1093.

My soul is going to kill me so it can get the hell out of here.

1094.

You can tell I'm in love when I put on my grandpa's old Halloween
costume and run around like a crazy person.

1095.

I like the sun. I also like drum circles that consist mostly
of little boys.

1096.

I saw a snake.

1097.

Fire is awesome. Show it some respect.

1098.

Women are like leaves, in that they gossip and turn bright colors
when they die.

1099.

I could see this bird, but then it got dark and I couldn't
see it anymore.

1100.

Last night was kind of boring, except that my friend died and we played dress-up with her dead body.

1101.

Nature thinks all her weird creations are hilarious. The platypus, for example. Or flatulence. Or both at the same time.

1102.

I wish I could return to the magical land of childhood where dewdrops are like diamonds and it's always Wednesday. But not if it means going through puberty in reverse.

1103.

The perception of an object is a system of said object's commoditization.

1104.

It gradually became night through a process marked by crickets, hats being taken off, and the sun descending past the visible horizon.

1105.

Flirtatious Emily Dickinson is mad at austere, heartbroken Emily Dickinson.

1106.

Nature is a hotel without indoor plumbing or room service.

1107.

I think I'm turning into a butterfly?

1108.

I hate cleaning. Especially right after someone I love just died.

1109.

I'm probably the only person there is who exists.

1110.

Thanksgiving Day is lame.

1111.

I like God because he's a friend of mine who killed the original God and is now God.

1112.

When people realize God doesn't exist, God will die.

1113.

That guy has a really big face.

1114.

Sometimes I stop loving people. Sometimes I don't, Sue.

1115.

I like Heaven. I also like it when people tip their hat to me in the street. I like that very much indeed.

1116.

I prefer sunsets to the sun.

1117.

Death is over there again, petting his dead sheep. He's kind of weird but all in all a nice guy.

1118.

Some of my imaginary friends are imaginary
journalists who report on imaginary news to me that
some of my real friends don't believe.

1119.

Some abstract concepts are more important than others.
Importance, for example, is an important abstract concept.

1120.

You don't have to say thank you to say thank you.

1121.

This weather is terrible. Girl, you gotta dress that shit up.

1122.

During the spring, I can't not be sexually aroused.

1123.

I prefer liquor when I'm drinking it.

1124.

There are two scientific extremities. The infinitely large and the
infinitely small. People usually forget about the infinitely small.
Don't do that.

1125.

Paradise is being able to opt out of "Paradise."

1126.

I can't believe they just shot that bird. Those bastards.
I hope they enjoy Hell. I'm just kidding. I hope they don't
enjoy Hell but that they go there.

1127.

I am glad that days exist.

1128.

I'm in love with a long-distance runner.

1129.

I'm going to remain a virgin so that I taste better when
God decides to eat me.

1130.

The best way to stay alive is to seal yourself in an airtight
chamber until you die.

1131.

My favorite diamonds are expensive diamonds.

1132.

I wish I were a vampire.

1133.

Women are built to be baby-making machines.

1134.

Birds hate liars.

1135.

I wish I were made of diamonds.

1136.

I'd prefer to keep my soul.

1137.

Your mom is as cold and dry as a husk in winter.

1138.

I'm better and lonelier than you are.

1139.

Sorry, I lost track of the time, and now you're dead.

1140.

God is kind of clumsy.

1141.

Sometimes I eat roses. Because I'm fabulous.

1142.

The bugs that exist in the afterlife are extra creepy.

1143.

Sometimes I'm surprised that humans still remember how to make fire.

1144.

There's this old mansion just outside of town where squatters and teenagers go to have sex. How do I know about it? Don't ask.

1145.

When I'm dead, you'll be dead to me.

1146.

Nighttime hates stars.

1147.

I'm too busy thinking about having sex with Sue to become famous.

1148.

William Tell was kind of an asshole.

1149.

Places have short attention spans.

1150.

All beetles are terrorists.

1151.

He likes it when I'm on top during sex.

1152.

Sometimes the wind goes crazy.

1153.

You'll feel better in the morning. Or else you won't.
Anyway, time doesn't really care about you, it being an abstract
concept without human qualities except those we force upon it.

1154.

My friend disappeared because he's magical! Oh, wait, he just died.

1155.

It's snowing. And that pleases me.

1156.

I'm sad that guy who used to wear that hat is dead.

1157.

Sometimes when I get drunk I wake up not knowing where I am.
It's like magic!

1158.

If a woman is good at math, she is probably a witch.

1159.

My mother can't come to the door because she is being cooked inside a green oven.

1160.

The wind has a really cushy job.

1161.

The citizens of Naples do not want to be destroyed by a volcano.

1162.

It's hard to access certain materials that are too deep in the ground to be accessed.

1163.

Spider webs don't remain structurally sound for long periods of time. But they're pretty.

1164.

It was not November, but it is now November.

1165.

I hope the last thing I say before I die isn't stupid.

1166.

Zombies don't like parades.

1167.

Nature just "scuttled my balloon."

1168.

Sometimes God has sex with the sun. Because he can.

1169.

I remember the day my friend died better than the day my friend
did not die.

1170.

I won't be truly satisfied until I find a flower big enough to fit
my entire body inside of it.

1171.

I like to watch people sleeping (a little too much).
Here's looking at you, Sue.

1172.

The best part about being in love is how your toes and your elbows
feel when you're in love.

1173.

I can't talk when I am around this guy because I'm in love with
him. I know this is not an original feeling, but it is.

1174.

There was a spider crawling on me and he made
me feel like a gymnasium on which the spider was
practicing for the spider Olympics.

1175.

Sometimes I feel small because infinity exists.

1176.

Mother Nature looks pretty normal but she's bat-shit crazy. She's really into juggling and necromancy.

1177.

I'm a virgin if you want me to be.

1178.

When it comes down to it, I prefer small, insignificant things, like humans, to God and Jesus and all those guys. They're kind of boring.

1179.

It's hard to be sad and to jump at the same time.

1180.

I hate when people tell the same jokes over and over.

1181.

I hate all ultimatums without exception.

1182.

I wish I were Time.

1183.

I'm pretty judgmental when it comes to my friends' girlfriends.

1184.

I hate meeting new people unless they're flowers.

1185.

She never struck me as fat, but I guess she is a little overweight.

1186.

I wish orgasms lasted longer. I'm just saying.

1187.

Sometimes I wonder if other people can hear me when
I'm screaming inside of my head.

1188.

I should probably see a doctor about my mental trauma
before it's too late.

1189.

It was kind of rude of God to pretend to be a human, just
so he could show us up at our own game.

1190.

Humans can survive more drastic shifts in weather than most
flowering plants can. Sorry, guys.

1191.

Happy Birthday. No, seriously. I'm actually glad you were born.

1192.

God knows what he's doing when he's fucking things up:
he's fucking things up, that's what he's doing.

1193.

February is fantastic.

1194.

March is okay. He's kind of weird. He wears purple shoes.
It might be a British thing.

1195.

You make me hate everybody else, Sue.

1196.

It's better to be a raving lunatic than a lunatic who doesn't
have anything to say.

1197.

I'm kind of amazing and modest.

1198.

I was really bored so I started talking to myself and then the time
just flew by.

1199.

Butterflies are really good at driving boats.
They just never get the chance to do it.

1200.

My friend's a slut. But, whatever, give her a break.

1201.

It's hard to find a good apartment when you're an abstract thought.

1202.

One should think optimistically about things. I'm not less happy
now that my friend died, I'm more unhappy.

1203.

I was in such a good mood until you gave me the finger.

1204.

I'm happiest when I'm most agoraphobic.

1205.

Zombies are a very honorable and proud race.

1206.

Remember when Jesus broke Paul and Silas out of jail?
That was awesome.

1207.

My personal currency doesn't have a very good exchange rate
at most banks.

1208.

Thieves just want to be loved.

1209.

I might be a zombie, but I still have to go to work.

1210.

You can believe in things you believe in if you do.

1211.

I'm really glad no one can hear what's going on inside of my head.
Have I said that already? Did I say it out loud?

1212.

After I got done slaughtering countless men on the battlefield,
I felt some remorse.

1213.

Men treat women like one of an endless number of sex receptacles.

1214.

Zombies are citizens of the only true democracy.

1215.

I like to watch my exes slowly grow older and more pathetic.

1216.

I wish I were a tornado in the arctic that no one saw
and then disappeared.

1217.

Now that I've eaten food it's hard to go back to eating only inedible
objects.

1218.

If your bones don't have marrow in them it's hard to survive.

1219.

I always eat before I go to a feast, so I can be like "No, I'm not
hungry. I already ate."

1220.

Collectively, the human race is a loud, obnoxious person.

1221.

People who are in love are statistically less likely to die.
You're killing me too slowly, Sue.

1222.

I am too familiar with the limits of happiness.

1223.

This life could have been enough if it were all that there were.
But it's not, so it's not.

1224.

Birds wouldn't function well as a system of currency, because they can fly, and they wouldn't fit inside of your wallet.

1225.

Oh, I didn't see you there.

1226.

There exists a moment in the time-space continuum in which my parents are constantly having sex. And it's gross.

1227.

I know this girl who has the biggest breasts in the world. She's really nice, she just has this huge rack that's kind of out of control.

1228.

I can't stop being into this guy even though he doesn't care about me.

1229.

I'm really bad at math on days when my friends die.

1230.

I'm going to fight myself to the death.

1231.

I can't believe that cold-hearted bitch didn't want to have sex with me. Oh, she's dead. I see.

1232.

Water is pretty durable.

1233.

I was happy until I was actually happy at which point
I wasn't happy.

1234.

I remember all kinds of useless shit.

1235.

I'm not afraid of swimming. I just don't like to get wet.

1236.

Little boys are kind of like puppies. I guess that makes
me an old, bitter cat.

1237.

Sometimes it's hard to see where I'm going and I stop so
I don't trip but it takes me longer to get to where I'm going
because I keep stopping.

1238.

The best way to break up your routine is by meeting a stranger and
getting them to kill you.

1239.

People look better when you can't see them.

1240.

There are a lot of turtles in Heaven.

1241.

Apples keep well.

1242.

I'm successful when it comes to failure.

1243.

It's hard to think of the right word to describe the right word.

1245.

Seconds are afraid of centuries because centuries want to eat them.

1246.

Sometimes when it rains, it's also very windy, and everything gets very wet until it stops raining. I should be a meteorologist.

1247.

I like being almost overwhelmed.

1248.

It was foggy, but then it wasn't.

1249.

If it hadn't just been sunny, I wouldn't want it to be sunny.

1250.

The idea of mortality carries with it the idea of the opposite of mortality.

1251.

At least Time tried really hard not to be an asshole, even though he failed.

1252.

I prefer sad, pathetic people.

1253.

I feel like a really fat person who thinks she isn't fat.

1254.

I want you to take my V-card.

1255.

I wish I were a mermaid.

1256.

I want Sue to eat me.

1257.

Birds build their nests out of twigs because they don't have a highly developed sense of architecture and construction.

1258.

I'm more of a swamp than a river.

1259.

People were always people when they were people.

1260.

I hope there are zombie doctors that can help me when I'm a zombie and I get sick.

1261.

There have always been shiny things.

1262.

Things are okay until you actually think about it.

DICKINSON, ASLEEP WITH HER EYES OPEN.

1263.

Abstract concepts require a medium like language to convey
that an abstraction like language exists.

1264.

I like my friends, but I don't like how they all decided to get old.

1265.

I enjoy abbreviations. That's why I enjoyed killing myself.
RIP, ED.

1266.

Our local preacher is an idiot. I don't think Jesus would like him
at all. Because he's stupid. And I don't like him.

1267.

I want to own more stuff.

1268.

The only thing bad writers are good for is spreading disease.

1269.

You're more likely to become fat if you have a big house.

1270.

I like to watch people when they are watching people.

1271.

I'm kind of a badass.

1272.

When I like a place, I pull out some of my hair and leave
it there as a marker.

1273.

Remembering the past is dangerous because the past might
shoot you in the face.

1274.

The worst part about breaking up with her is that she didn't die.

1275.

The ocean wants all Earth's water to itself.

1276.

I'm not sure about it, but sometimes I get the feeling that my
soul wants to eat me.

1277.

It's hard to argue with someone whose opinion is "No."

1278.

She looked so happy that I wanted to die.

1279.

I regret not doing the things I wanted to do.

1280.

God and Jesus are kind of cliquish.

1281.

I would be happier if people like Sue would stop
stopping loving me.

1282.

It's hard to be hopeful if you have even a remotely
developed sense of critical thinking.

1283.

I'm a bad driver because I enjoy leaving things to chance.

1284.

I would love to be a pirate almost as much as I would love being forced to walk the plank.

1285.

I saw this bird pick up a twig, and I could tell that it was the best bird that ever existed.

1286.

A book is a good means of transportation even though it might actually sink if you try to ride one like a boat.

1287.

Sometimes it's hard being so powerful.

1288.

My friend knows how to levitate.

1289.

Zombie children are a little creepier than zombie adults.

1290.

You could spend your whole life thinking. And you do.

1291.

It's easier to think you're famous than to actually be famous.

1292.

I won't live very long and even that I'll do helplessly.

1293.

If you leave me for a day, you might as well just kill me.

1294.

Sometimes I plan on doing something and then I don't do it.

1295.

I understand solids but sometimes I confuse liquids with gases.

1296.

My friend's favorite thing to do is to steal things.

1297.

Bees aren't usually afraid of heights.

1298.

When I like someone, I don't usually do anything about it.

1299.

I hope your lips last forever.

1300.

I like hearing stuff.

1301.

Once you run out of room in your brain, you don't really need to do anything.

1302.

I like things that exist almost as much as I like things that don't.

1303.

People who have opinions are assholes.

1304.

When you get old, things tend to fall off your body.

1305.

People collect butterflies, but they don't usually collect dead flies.

1306.

Zombies can't wait for famous people to die so they can
be famous zombies.

1307.

I like this girl even though she's kind of awkward and mean.
And married to my brother.

1308.

The best way to break my heart is to run me over with a blimp.

1309.

White female seeking zombie. About me: I enjoy confined spaces
and summer. Please respond.

1310.

I'm thinking about having my eyes removed. I need a change.

1311.

God is anorexic.

1312.

Crickets are stupid.

1313.

I like September because everyone gets very serious.
I'm a pretty serious person.

1314.

God doesn't have a time machine.

1315.

When I'm dead I'm going to start a zombie noise band.

1316.

If you only knew.

1317.

I hate trying on new clothes.

1318.

There's nothing better than some dirty gossip.

1319.

I think spring will happen again this year.

1320.

Don't let April in. He's trying to kill March.

1321.

Islands are mountains that aren't mountains anymore.

1322.

My soul wishes it had someone to make out with.

1323.

Sometimes I forget about the Earth when I'm looking at someone's face, especially if the face is sad. Or Sue's.

1324.

I prefer medium salsa to mild salsa.

1325.

I'm afraid of being alive.

1326.

Sometimes things don't work out as you planned. Like that time
I found out that bitch was cheating on me.

1327.

A lot of people will be alive.

1328.

It's unlikely that the human race will last very long by any
standards unless they become zombies.

1329.

Butterflies are better than people. That's just how it is.

1330.

The hornier you are, the less power you have in the structure
of your relationship.

1331.

My heart wanted to visit you, so it left, and now I'm having a hard
time circulating blood throughout my body.

1332.

Isaac must have had some serious daddy issues.

1333.

If Caesar came back from the dead and tried to start a conversation
with me, I would probably run away.

1334.

I'm glad I don't know that I don't have any friends.

1335.

Useful things aren't as pretty as useless things.

1336.

Queen Elisabeth is a no-frills kind of gal.

1337.

I'm getting pretty old, and I miss you, Sue.

1338.

Sad people are stupid.

1339.

Jesus is nice, but Satan wants it more.

1340.

Guess what? Summer's an asshole.

1341.

Guess what? Autumn is an even bigger asshole than summer.

1342.

I'm pretty sure Moses was a zombie.

1343.

More people want drugs than have access to them.

1344.

Jesus never knows when he's outworn his welcome.

1345.

There are many reasons why I'm pathetic. One of which is the way
I pretend that you love me.

1346.

I'm sending you a dead flower. I don't know why anymore.

1347.

At all times, I'm pretty sure something's going to happen.

1348.

You can tell a bird is a bobolink when it's awesome. And you can
tell a bird is awesome if it's a bobolink.

1349.

I'm proud to be ashamed of myself.

1350.

Mushrooms are cute.

1351.

Women get the shit end of the stick.

1352.

I'm sleepy but I'm also mad that I'm sleepy.

1353.

I'm really loud during sex.

1354.

Do what you want. Whatever. (I do what I want.)

1355.

Frogs are also bad at interior decorating.

1356.

I hate clowns.

1357.

I like my clitoris. Clitorises are great.

1358.

The real estate market is better if you are very small.

1359.

Humans usually stay human.

1360.

I don't like money but I like gold.

1361.

Everything's better when you're naked. Take Sue, for example.

1362.

I only want superpowers so I can feel important.

1363.

Zombies are good at getting people's attention.

1364.

I'm glad I can get the hell out of here even if I'm not going to.

1365.

I liked being a baby.

1366.

Another sunrise. Sometimes I wish the sun would
just make up its mind and set already.

1367.

Old people have cute faces.

1368.

I'm afraid of orgasms.

1369.

Rats don't care. (They do what they want.)

1370.

Is that all there is, Sue?

1371.

Nature is pathetic.

1372.

I don't understand evaporation.

1373.

I feel bad for spiders because nobody wants to hold their hands.

1374.

I like winter, because it isn't currently winter.

1375.

I'm sad that I'm not happy.

1376.

The moon is Buddhist.

1377.

Happiness is a trap.

1378.

I'm a dirty little tramp.

1379.

I wonder what the newspaper industry will do when humans are extinct. Zombies don't like to read newspapers.

1380.

August reminds me of July.

1381.

The brain is the center of the nervous system in all vertebrate, and most invertebrate, animals. I like my brain.

1382.

I don't like boring people because they're always plating the residue of Adz with monotony.

1383.

Birds hate ornithologists.

1384.

My brain is a parasite.

1385.

If you remember too much, you will implode.

1386.

Nobody cares that I got the perfect attendance award.

1387.

Robert E. Lee was an asshole, but at least he was dedicated to being an asshole.

1388.

Sure, she's pretty. Too bad she has a midwestern accent.

1389.

The birds and the bees can't wait to dance on our graves.

1390.

Time will probably exist until the end of time.

1391.

I'm going to sue God for malpractice.

1392.

Love whines a lot.

1393.

There are small cows crawling across my eye.

1394.

Sometimes after listening to frogs, I feel a little drunk.

1395.

Butterflies are always overdressed.

1396.

I can see farther through a telescope than I can see normally.

1397.

Ugly, pathetic people probably find you really attractive.

1398.

The Earth is famous.

1399.

The sun is extremely judgmental.

1400.

Humans are worthless, except when they are having a parade.

1401.

Waking up feels like suddenly being thrown into
a pile of raw meat.

1402.

Zombies are usually pretty emo.

1403.

They're all going to laugh at you.

1404.

I forget where I have to go to be happy.

1405.

Things matter even if they don't matter all the time.

1406.

Now that my friend died, I think that I should act like nothing
happened and treat him like a normal person, even if he is a
little smelly and is slowly shedding pieces of his body in a gradual
process of decomposition.

1407.

Squirrels have the best parties.

1408.

Bats are weird-looking on purpose.

1409.

I wish I had minions.

1410.

The wind is nature's stylist.

1411.

If summer were a person, she would be the kind of person whose
hat I want to steal.

1412.

Animals are good at physics, astronomy, geology,
and mathematics. But I have the upper hand when it
comes to the liberal arts.

1413.

Fetuses have no idea what they're getting into.

1414.

The trees hate us for eating so many of their babies.

1415.

I forget about things when things are happening.

1416.

The sunset doesn't look like a singular thing.

1417.

I think tomorrow is going to happen, but I've been wrong before.

1418.

The sun is in an abusive relationship with the sky.

1419.

I eat happiness.

1420.

Atheists have more fun. They can go to Hell.

1421.

Jesus thinks he knows everything.

1422.

Happiness is a closeted homosexual.

1423.

In the spring, I turn into a mermaid.

1424.

I have hope but only involuntarily.

1425.

Sometimes I follow people around, smiling at them, in case
of the remote possibility that they might want me to follow them
around, staring at them and smiling creepily.

1426.

Bees enjoy fuzzy things. Luckily, there is an endless supply
of said fuzzy things.

1427.

Naked people will also die.

1428.

I really like this guy Jesus. I don't know if you've heard of him.
He's kind of obscure.

1429.

I feel bad about talking trash about my dead friend named Katie.

1430.

I hate her pretty little face.

1431.

Sometimes when I'm hanging out with my friend, our brains come out of our heads.

1432.

I'm boring because I love you.

1433.

Wells are great because there is a lot of water in wells that you can drink.

1434.

Shut up already if you're dead.

1435.

I'm offended that I have to live on the Earth because it is so much better than me.

1436.

I want my sister-in-law, Sue, to be my sex slave.

1437.

You're covered in skin, and that's gross.

1438.

I like to run, especially when I'm running away from something in terror.

1439.

No one is worthy of my friend's glorious boobs.

1440.

Humans love being stupid.

1441.

The wind is manic-depressive.

1442.

Sometimes the sun looks angry because it wants to destroy us.
At these times, it is also very pretty.

1443.

I wish I could build a house out of a sticky substance that I excrete
from my body.

1444.

You could tell she was royalty by the way she coughed.

1445.

I'm famous because I didn't want to be famous.

1446.

I love waterbeds.

1447.

I want to be insane so I can be happy.

1448.

I can totally fly. I just don't feel like it right now.

1449.

Sometimes, even though I'm Christian, I find death
a little unattractive.

1450.

I wonder why God hates me enough to pair every small joy
I have with a distinctly impalpable sense of desperation.
The next time I see him, I'm going to tell him he's an asshole.

1451.

It's hard to stop remembering things.

1452.

God's an elitist.

1453.

My friend who is dead has a gravestone that notes her date of birth
and death and that will probably outlast any actual memory of her.

1454.

Opals are really in fashion this season.

1455.

There's a little zombie inside each and every one of us.

1456.

If language could repudiate the physical world,
then neither could exist.

1457.

Autumn is bizarro summer.

1458.

Stasis is a sort of creation.

1459.

The basis of religion is structurally flawed, at best.

1460.

Most zombies are homeless. Like God.

1461.

I would've liked Duchamp if I had lived into the twentieth century.

1462.

The fastest way to die is to be a good person.

1463.

I miss my mom sometimes because I love her.

1464.

Love is a bitch named Susan Gilbert Dickinson.

1465.

Nice people are more likely to commit infanticide.

1466.

People who love more than one person are shallow.

1467.

When it's hot, I'd rather be in the shade. Or else be dead.

1468.

Faith is as replaceable as an imaginary button.

1469.

The afterlife is sort of like Amherst meets Antarctica.

1470.

Death is someone I want to have sex with but only
after we're married.

1471.

Now that my friend's dead we can sell his organs.

1472.

If you're going to get the sun a present, you should get him some lava. He loves lava.

1473.

I hate waiting for the train.

1474.

I just saw either a vampire or a werewolf. Probably a werewolf.

1475.

Don't be mean or people will kill themselves and it will be partially your fault.

1476.

The vast majority of my thoughts are completely idiotic.

1477.

I don't want to have sex until I'm moments away from dying of old age. Then I'll know I'm ready.

1478.

Chirp.

1479.

I always break stuff when I'm happy.

1480.

She's been dead for ten years, and she's still pretty sexy (for a zombie).

1481.

God wants me to take my clothes off.

1482.

I like to eat things that are inedible. Like Sue.

1483.

I'm going to die soon, because humans don't live very long.
I don't know. It sucks.

1484.

Spring is like a person yelling to himself in the woods.

1485.

Even when Jesus was dying, he knew how to have a party.

1486.

Reincarnation doesn't really match the New England aesthetic.

1487.

Belshazzar doesn't have a pen pal.

1488.

Orioles are made primarily of gold. I don't care if that doesn't
make scientific sense.

1489.

Everything is a little bubbly today.

1490.

I like to blow the seeds off of dandelions. It feels like
I'm decapitating people.

1491.

Poetry aspires to experience.

1492.

Flowers are ferocious when it comes to pollination.

1493.

Hope has a slow metabolism.

1494.

Real secrets can't be spoken.

1495.

I'd rather have the sun explode than be lied to.

1496.

Beauty pisses me off.

1497.

Zombies aren't good at finance.

1498.

Time hates you.

1499.

God doesn't care what heinous crime you commit as long as you blush while you're doing it.

1500.

I'm sorry you're an asshole, God. It's probably my fault.

1501.

I like when people say nice things.

1502.

Lightning is actually caused by magical creatures.

1503.

It's hard to ride an imaginary boat in a real sea.

1504.

When you rape and pillage a town you should feel pleased but also a little guilty.

1505.

The trees want to kill the sky, but sometimes they take a break from their constant war to just hang out.

1506.

Sometimes when we look at each other I feel like we're talking even though we're not.

1507.

I want to be famous and on fire.

1508.

Apparently old people have feelings too.

1509.

No one likes rich people who aren't in love.

1510.

Satan isn't very good at home ec.

1511.

I like music because it's quite possibly evil.

1512.

If hope were a building it would collapse.

1513.

I'm excited that I will eventually become air.

1514.

People always talk shit about zombies.

1515.

Unfortunately, you're beautiful whether you
want to be or not, Sue.

1516.

I like someone who doesn't like me again.

1517.

True physicists hate love.

1518.

I'm sad it's not Christmas anymore.

1519.

Sometimes when I'm about to kill someone and they beg
for their life I don't kill them.

1520.

Birds are working-class angels.

1521.

God prefers people who have shiny faces.

1522.

All kinds of things enjoy living underground, eating dead bodies.

1523.

Caterpillars are quiet.

1524.

If people could visit the afterworld, no one would stay on Earth.

1525.

Mines don't have wings.

1526.

I find it hard to love people after I've had sex with them.

1527.

She seems happier now that she's a corpse.

1528.

I feel like I haven't had an orgasm in years. Oh shit, here it comes.

1529.

God is stalking me because he wants to have sex with me.

1530.

I didn't realize how tall the guy who lived next door
was until he died.

1531.

I was too shy to tell this girl I liked her, and now she's dead.
This always happens to me.

1532.

I wish I didn't have to join God's army of zombies.

1533.

Your name is shiny. Sue.

1534.

I wish I didn't care about how much I don't care about things.

1535.

I had a friend but she became feral.

1536.

I don't know how to remember things, but I remember
remembering how I used to remember.

1537.

Angels don't have bodies but sometimes it looks like they do.
And sometimes when they're pretending to have bodies they forget
to pretend to have a nose or eyes and they look kind of off.

1538.

Baby Jesus was probably quite the gentleman.

1539.

I feel like a better person now that this person I don't like is dying.

1540.

Guns hate stars, and I love America.

1541.

Fuck, it's my birthday yet again.

1542.

Struggling to survive is a little shameful.

1543.

I feel bad that everyone likes flowers but no one likes flower stems.
I like flower stems.

1544.

Crows are pretty emo (like zombies).

1545.

Zombies love spring even though they kind of stick out
like a sore thumb when they're in a field of flowers and bluebirds,
swinging their arms, singing their zombie songs about Jesus,
king of the zombies.

1546.

Sometimes when people pretend to be dead,
they're not pretending.

1547.

Bees party like it's their job (which it is).

1548.

If there were the absence of everything, it would be everything.

1549.

I know this little boy zombie who rides a zombie cow.

1550.

I prefer babies to dead people.

1551.

Sex is a war.

1552.

You are either famous or oblivion.

1553.

Some people don't like it when criminals escape from prison.
But look how happy it makes them.

1554.

Souls are nice, but they're also stupid.

1555.

The best way to catch a horse is with a gun.

1556.

Have I mentioned that wizards never sleep?

1557.

Love is stupid and so am I.

1558.

Blood is good at some things but not at dancing.

1559.

I'm kind of getting tired of naming all the things that I prefer
to people, but while I'm at it: butterflies.

1560.

I know what happens to summer: the days get shorter, and then
it isn't summer anymore.

1561.

I'm not sure if I should hang out with my friend, even though she
definitely knows how to have good time. (She's a little slutty.)

1562.

Have I mentioned that bees like to party?

1563.

New England is not tropical.

1564.

Some things don't come back, and most things don't want to.
Maybe it's me?

1565.

Dandelions hate death.

1566.

I'm afraid to know things like knowing that I'm afraid
to know things.

1567.

God is somewhere or not.

1568.

I want the little pirate that lives inside of my heart to be my friend.

1569.

I love Orion.

1570.

Stones like being stones.

1571.

Asterisks are stars too.

1572.

If I were a tree, I would want birds to have sex in me.

1573.

Jesus got to keep himself when he died.

1574.

Screw Heaven, I want to live on the moon.

1575.

I hope God still likes you if you turn into a zombie.

1576.

Saints are good at making renovations around the home.

1577.

The bible is about: dead people, ghosts, Bethlehem, Eden,
Satan (who was awesome), Judas (who was an asshole),
David (who was pretty cool), and gay people.

1578.

It was nice running into you, Sue, because you make me happy.

1579.

People who are seventy years old don't have as many friends
as younger people.

1580.

You have to be very round to be the sun.

1581.

Someone cut off God's hand, and the he bled to death,
so he doesn't exist anymore.

1582.

Ghosts are usually very courteous.

1583.

Happiness is phallic.

1584.

The last thing I'm going to say before I die is
"I don't know what to say."

1585.

I want to eat a small person and to have him grow to adulthood
inside of me.

1586.

The only thing there is in Heaven is a giant cardinal. It's pretty and
all, but kind of limited.

1587.

I don't like it when God gets bossy.

1588.

Death is just there. He doesn't hate you. He's just presenting you
with an option. That's it…

1589.

I'm a little emo.

1590.

I have a fear of guests and of death.

1591.

Sometimes birds exist and I can see them.

1592.

I wish I were a little less New Englandy and lame.

1593.

I would like to fly around like an evil monster,
slowly eating the entire planet.

1594.

Things that are alive are.

1595.

I think I hurt Jesus's feelings when I said that I hated him.

1596.

Jays are the best kind of birds. (Don't tell the bobolinks.)

1597.

I like hanging out with her, but the last time I got too close to her my arm caught on fire.

1598.

Daylight savings time was invented by wizards.

1599.

The sunset happened again.

1600.

Fact: sometimes angels turn into birds in order to spy on us.

1601.

Fiction: I'm worthy of the smallest level of engagement necessary to produce a memory in another human being.

1602.

I don't like unfortunate people like myself.

1603.

Some zombies have wings.

1604.

I went to visit this tree, but he told me he wasn't there.

1605.

Jesus only has a few hobbies. One of them
is collecting flying babies.

1606.

Gay people should come out of the closet.

1607.

Dear Sue: How come you haven't yet responded to the letter
I sent you yesterday?

1608.

I don't want to be charming. I want to be gruff and treated
on an equal level as men.

1609.

If you don't like Earth, you probably won't like Heaven.

1610.

If roses don't like you, I don't like you.

1611.

Stupid people are the human manifestation of the
third law of thermodynamics.

1612.

I'm a witch!

1613.

I like to think about things.

1614.

Memory lasts longer than cake and flowers.

1615.

Flowers don't give a shit.

1616.

The person who was once a baby named Emily Dickinson
will eventually die.

1617.

Jesus wants me to hang out with him and his gang of winged
babies. He says he knows how to have a good time.

1618.

Even though the wind is strong enough to make a noise by
traveling through different geographical features fast enough to
cause vibrations to occur against the plants and buildings and other
obstacles that it passes, establishing sound waves that operate on
a frequency within the range of the human ear's perception, it will
probably not destroy the Earth.

1619.

Summer came to the funeral dressed like a drunk whore.

1620.

I miss my friend, the bobolink, and how he used to make fun
of the Presbyterians with me.

1621.

Sunsets aren't for everyone. That's actually my sunset.

1622.

I feel bad that I didn't fully appreciate summer this year.
I'm sorry, summer. Come back.

1623.

In humans, hearts have two atriums and two ventricles that pump blood throughout the greater circulatory system.

1624.

Something was confusing, but you figured it out. Good job.

1625.

When you die, I'm going to stand by your dead body and follow it wherever it goes. Deal with it, Sue.

1626.

Everything runs by the law of supply and demand.

1627.

Some things can't be penetrated.

1628.

I like Heaven because I'm into bondage.

1629.

It's hard to speak without using your mouth.

1630.

I like flies but only because they remind me of bumblebees.

1631.

I don't miss my friend, but I do miss certain parts of her body.

1632.

Birds miss their dead bird-children.

1633.

Bees are surrealists.

1634.

I'm slowly being eaten by zombies.

1635.

My friend drank some poison and now he's dead.

1636.

If you want to have everything, you have to be a slut.

1637.

I'm a procrastinator.

1638.

I'm afraid of water but only when it stops to look at me.

1639.

I'm secretly a zombie. And I can fly.

1640.

When the Holy Spirit wants to have sex with me, he does.

1641.

God starts fires. He doesn't put them out.

1642.

Another one of my friends died. I miss my dead friends.

1643.

The sea is better than me.

1644.

People look better at sunset because you can't see them as well.

1645.

I enjoy having multiple orgasms. With multiple Sues.

1646.

Jesus wanted to be a lumberjack.

1647.

I can't find something that I'm looking for because
I don't know what it looks like.

1648.

Zombies have small feet, so they wear little boots.

1649.

I'm going to drag your dead body from its grave and bring it back
to life so you can be my girlfriend.

1650.

Bees don't get into heated debates unless you bring up flowers.

1651.

Balloons hate the Earth.

1652.

I wish I could either stop time, go back in time, or travel to
a parallel dimension at will.

1653.

Heaven doesn't use the metric system.

1654.

It's hard to make conversations be important when they should be.

1655.

My pet peeve is when people describe
how trees look in summer.

1656.

It's weird that I can't hear the Sun.

1657.

Mother Nature is a lesbian. And proud of it.

1658.

Sue, you are my BFF. And when we're dead we can be DBFFs.

1659.

People have a tendency to kill things they love.

1660.

Zombies have really terrible accents.

1661.

Heart attacks are often caused by stress.

1662.

All children want to be sorceresses, but it's not really that great being a sorceress if you're a lonely sorceress.

1663.

Birds aren't very good at horseback riding.

1664.

The colors that exist inside a prism don't really exist inside the prism, but they kind of do?

1665.

When I got hit by lightning, it gave me a feeling of satisfaction.

1666.

You live longer if you're sneaky.

1667.

"I knew I loved you before I met you.
I think I dreamed you into life."

1668.

God likes to kill flowers. Again: what an asshole.

1669.

Man, it sure is great being a zombie.

1670.

Animals hate winter. Chestnuts, on the other hand, love it.

1671.

Can I pay for this with orgasms? Oh, I can't? Fine, I'll just keep
them to myself.

1672.

The USPS doesn't deliver to Heaven. That makes the gods sad.

1673.

Sometimes stars are not large gaseous bodies.
Sometimes they are symbols.

1674.

I want to have sex with you in the sea, on the land, and in the air.
And with my sister-in-law. On a hovercraft.

1675.

The Earth is God's prison. I want to extend my sentence.

1676.

I like rebels.

1677.

I don't need to have good manners to have a good time.

1678.

The world is X-rated.

1679.

Drunk people are to ditches as babies are to cribs.

1680.

As much as I love being confused, I would give it all up to be
a boring, one-note goddess.

1681.

If I owned a navy, I would drink a lot and wage a fantastic,
bloody war.

1682.

I want to have sex with you because you're an angel, and then I can
blackmail you into getting me into Heaven.

1683.

It doesn't matter where you go or what you do. Something
probably matters, but I don't know what it is.

1684.

Human love is almost as good as zombie love.

1685.

My friend died. Suddenly everything sucks forever.

1686.

Hypothetical situations engender actualities.

1687.

Everyone's so pretty. I find that very annoying.

1688.

The more endangered an animal is, the more delicious it is.

1689.

I like to like things to myself.

1690.

My new roommate, Infinity, is a real downer.

1691.

New England is like a dead volcano.

1692.

I like morning when it's not happening.

1693.

Summer reminds me of autumn. Autumn reminds me of winter.
It's June, and everything will eventually die.

1694.

I like quiet sex.

1695.

You look better now that you're a zombie. Did you lose weight?

1696.

Ghosts are lonely ghosts.

1697.

Seasons transition.

1698.

Night usually happens on time.

1699.

I live dangerously and indoors.

1700.

I want to be a celebrity in Heaven.

1701.

Butterflies are just a little garish.

1702.

Don't eat famous-people food. You will die.

1703.

I don't trust Austrians.

1704.

I know plenty of zombies who would give their right hand
to be alive again, if they had one.

1705.

Winter has a lot in common with Finland.

1706.

Another one of my friends died. I wish I could touch her, but they
hid her dead body from me, because I kept touching it.

1707.

Justice isn't real justice until you torture the truth out of her.

1708.

You live really far away, but I want to see you.

1709.

The sun set again.

1710.

I like to look at dead people's faces.

1711.

My friend died in his sleep, and now I don't know what he's doing.

1712.

When I'm dead, they'll probably find out that I was a witch.

1713.

Goodbye, autumn. Go home.

1714.

You are going to die. And it will be awesome.

1715.

Sometimes I try to eat words, and it doesn't really work out.

1716.

When people forget me, I feel like shit.

1717.

I don't like it when people don't like me as much as I like them.

1718.

God is a terrible landlord.

1719.

Be nice or someone might kill you.

1720.

Winter is okay if you winterize.

1721.

Only stupid people don't have time machines,
and I don't have one.

1722.

Nature believes in the power of negative capability.

1723.

Sometimes I get confused by mannequins.

1724.

Zombies won't die because they're stubborn.

1725.

I'm happy because I don't know why I'm happy.

1726.

You're not allowed to kill yourself. Sorry.

1727.

Sometimes people love each other sometimes, Sue.

1728.

Although curiosity is a human idea,
it occurs more often in nature than in humans.

1729.

I want to surprise myself.
Maybe I'll shoot myself in the head.

1730.

The man who I met who had a
Hula-Hoop can't get pregnant.

1731.

You would probably be the same person you
are even if you didn't have hands or feet.

1732.

Zombies are usually really stoned.

1733.

Sometimes the sky isn't blue. Sometimes it is yellow.

1734.

Paradise is outdated.

1735.

Storms are charming. Except I'm being sarcastic.

1736.

I guess I'm glad I'm alive.

1737.

I can't wait until I don't care about anything anymore.

1738.

When I die I want to be buried in lotion.

1739.

I'm lame, because I'm not a bird.

1740.

Children make dying people sad.

1741.

The Wizard of Oz is a metaphor for death.

1742.

I dreamt about a worm that turned into a snake. I guess I'm afraid
of penises. If only Sue were afraid of my brother's.

1743.

I'm a nice volcano.

1744.

God always trashes my apartment when he comes over.

1745.

I only want to date broken-down, jaded people.

1746.

Summer orgasms for about three months straight.
God, I need a vacation.

1747.

Certain body parts fit inside of certain other body parts
better than others.

1748.

Tomorrow exists as an idea but not as a thing.

1749.

I can see better when I can't see things very well because
I try harder to see things.

1750.

Sometimes I pretend that sad things are funny,
even when they're not. Ha.

1751.

Sometimes I don't wear a belt, because I'm crazy like that.

1752.

God is a jealous Janice.

1753.

I wish cups came in bottomless-cup sizes.

1754.

I don't know where which part of me is.

1755.

I think I saw a ghost. Ghosts are the same color as semen.

1756.

It's hard to be sad when you're having an orgasm.

1757.

What's the deal with immortality?

1758.

Love is a tired, old witch named Sue.

1759.

Man, I would not want to be Pontius Pilate.
Because he's burning in hell.

1760.

You're pathetic. Because you dumped me.

1761.

Life only tastes like candy because death doesn't.

1762.

Happiness is edible.

1763.

If I'm in love with you, watch out. Just ask Sue's therapist.

1764.

Bumblebees are better people than both people and dead people.

1765.

Umbrellas are useful. Parasols are useful if you're a whore.

1766.

Some zombies live underwater. They mostly eat fish.

1767.

Happy people are stupid.

1768.

Sometimes I just want to be bossed around.

1769.

Dead people are good at being dead.

1770.

Remembering sucks.

1771.

Fuck winter. I want it to be summer forever.

1772.

Children have child-sized troubles.

1773.

I don't want to go to hell.

1774.

Some people look like they want to beat you to death with
their face.

1775.

Moms don't like it when you kill their children.

1776.

I am secretly immortal. Now that I've told you I will have to kill
you unless you are secretly immortal too.

1777.

My friend died. I'm definitely not upset right now.
No, everything's just fine. Do I seem upset? Because I'm not.

1778.

I met this bird. I thought he was very nice.

1779.

A little bit of clover reminds me of lots of clover.

1780.

Vaginas are great.

1781.

I was friends with this one person, but then they changed.
They didn't talk to me anymore and got really flaky and then
started to decompose. So we're not friends anymore.

1782.

Zombies don't like ornithology.

1783.

If you know your friend is going to die, you should kill them.

1784.

Nobody will come to my zombie tea parties.

1785.

Now that I'm dead, my body is dead too.

1786.

Who misses who more? Me or my dead friend? Probably my dead friend misses me more than I miss him.

1787.

If nature were a person, she would like to travel with you. It's now or never, Sue. There's a ticket to Italy on your nightstand. I'll be waiting for you down by the docks. Wear something sexy.

1788.

Fame is ultimately useless I hope.

1789.

I almost wish I were deaf, so I wouldn't have to hear birds ever again. So I wouldn't have to hear birds and think of death. So I wouldn't have to face this terribly immediate association I have of beauty with death.

DICKINSON, DRESSED AS EMILY DICKINSON.

INDEX *by* THEME

INDEX *by* FIRST LINE

379. The Grass so little has to do,
380. All the letters I can write
381. I cannot dance opon my Toes—
382. Good Morning—Midnight—
383. I like to see it lap the Miles—
384. It dont sound so terrible—quite— as it did—
385. I'll clutch—and clutch—
386. Taking up the fair Ideal,
387. The Moon is distant from the Sea—
388. It would never be Common— more—I said—
389. Me—Come! My dazzled face
390. Do People moulder equally,
391. Knows how to forget!
392. We talked as Girls do—
393. Empty my Heart, of Thee—
394. I cried at Pity—not at Pain—
395. The face I carry with me—last—
396. I took one Draught of Life—
397. A train went through a burial gate,
398. The Morning after Wo—
399. Departed—to the Judgment—
400. I think the Hemlock likes to stand
401. Dare you see a Soul at the "White Heat"?
402. To hear an Oriole sing
403. I reason, Earth is short—
404. To put this World down, like a Bundle—
405. Although I put away his life—
406. Over and over, like a Tune—
407. One need not be a Chamber—to be Haunted—
408. Like some Old fashioned Miracle
409. The Soul selects her own Society—
410. How sick—to wait—in any place— but thine—
411. Mine—by the Right of the White Election!
412. She lay as if at play
413. Heaven is so far of the Mind
414. Inconceivably solemn!
415. More Life—went out—when He went
416. The Months have ends—the Years—a knot—
417. Removed from Accident of Loss
418. Your Riches—taught me—Poverty.
419. A Toad, can die of Light—
420. There are two Ripenings—
421. It ceased to hurt me, though so slow
422. Give little Anguish—
423. The first Day's Night had come—
424. The Color of the Grave is Green—
425. 'Twas like a Maelstrom, with a notch,
426. I gave Myself to Him—
427. Sunset at Night—is natural—
428. We grow accustomed to the Dark—
429. You'll know it—as you know 'tis Noon—
430. A Charm invests a face
431. If I may have it, when it's dead,
432. I read my sentence—steadily—
433. A Murmur in the Trees—to note—
434. It is dead—Find it—
435. Not in this World to see his face—
436. I found the words to every thought
437. I never felt at Home—Below—
438. The Body grows without—
439. I had been hungry, all the Years—
440. I Years had been from Home

625. Forget! The lady with the Amulet

626. Undue Significance a starving man attaches

627. I think I was enchanted

628. 'Tis Customary as we part

629. The Battle fought between the Soul

630. The Soul's Superior instants

631. Me prove it now—Whoever doubt

632. To lose One's faith—surpass

633. I saw no Way—The Heavens were stitched—

634. Had I presumed to hope—

635. Just to be Rich

636. It struck me—every Day—

637. I went to thank Her—

638. The Future never spoke—

639. I gained it so—

640. Death sets a Thing significant

641. What I can do—I will—

642. There is a flower that Bees prefer—

643. A Secret told—

644. For Death—or rather

645. Exhiliration—is within—

646. 'Tis One by One—the Father counts—

647. To fill a Gap

648. I've seen a Dying Eye

649. No Rack can torture me—

650. Death is potential to that Man

651. Smiling back from Coronation

652. That I did always love

653. No Crowd that has occurred

654. Beauty—be not caused—It Is—

655. He parts Himself—like Leaves—

656. I started Early—Took my Dog—

657. Endow the Living—with the Tears—

658. 'Tis true—They shut me in the Cold—

659. The Province of the Saved

660. I took my Power in my Hand—

661. Some such Butterfly be seen

662. I had no Cause to be awake—

663. I fear a Man of frugal speech—

664. Rehearsal to Ourselves

665. The Martyr Poets—did not tell—

666. I cross till I am weary

667. Answer July

668. There is a Shame of Nobleness—

669. An ignorance a Sunset

670. One Crucifixion is recorded—only—

671. The Sweetest Heresy received

672. Take Your Heaven further on—

673. A Tongue—to tell Him I am true!

674. I could not prove the Years had feet—

675. What Soft—Cherubic Creatures—

676. You know that Portrait in the Moon—

677. Funny—to be a Century—

678. Not probable—The barest Chance—

679. When Night is almost done—

680. Triumph—may be of several kinds—

681. Dont put up my Thread & Needle—

682. So well that I can live without—

683. At leisure is the Soul

684. Sweet—safe—Houses—

685. Glee—The great storm is over—

686. It makes no difference abroad—

687. I asked no other thing—

688. To know just how He suffered—would be dear—

689. It was too late for Man—

230

231

815. To this World she returned
816. I could not drink it, Sweet,
817. This Consciousness that is aware
818. Given in Marriage unto Thee
819. The Luxury to apprehend
820. The only news I know
821. Wert Thou but ill—that I might show thee
822. Midsummer, was it, when They died—
823. The first Day that I was a Life
824. A nearness to Tremendousness—
825. "Unto Me"? I do not know you—
826. Denial—is the only fact
827. All forgot for recollecting
828. Had I not This, or This, I said,
829. Between My Country—and the Others—
830. The Admirations—and Contempts—of time—
831. Till Death—is narrow Loving—
832. 'Tis Sunrise—little Maid—Hast Thou
833. Pain—expands the Time—
834. Fitter to see Him, I may be
835. He who in Himself believes—
836. Color—Caste —Denomination—
837. I make His Crescent fill or lack—
838. Robbed by Death—but that was easy—
839. Unfulfilled to Observation—
840. Love—is that later Thing than Death—
841. Struck, was I, nor yet by Lightning—
842. Patience—has a quiet Outer—
843. It bloomed and dropt, a Single Noon—

844. This Merit hath the Worst—
845. We can but follow to the Sun—
846. A Drop fell on the Apple Tree—
847. Her final Summer was it—
848. Who Giants know, with lesser Men
849. By my Window have I for Scenery
850. Defrauded I a Butterfly—
851. "I want"—it pleaded—All it's life—
852. It was a Grave, yet bore no Stone
853. She staked Her Feathers—Gained an Arc—
854. Despair's advantage is achieved
855. Two—were immortal twice—
856. I play at Riches—to appease
857. She rose to His Requirement—dropt
858. Time feels so vast that were it not
859. Who Court obtain within Himself
860. No Notice gave She, but a Change—
861. They say that "Time assuages"—
862. On the Bleakness of my Lot
863. This Bauble was preferred of Bees—
864. A Plated Life—diversified
865. Expectation—is Contentment—
866. This Dust, and it's Feature—
867. I felt a Cleaving in my Mind—
868. Fairer through Fading—as the Day
869. What I see not, I better see—
870. None can experience stint
871. The hallowing of Pain
872. Deprived of other Banquet,
873. It is a lonesome Glee—
874. If Blame be my side—forfeit Me—
875. Purple—
876. To be alive—is Power—
877. The Loneliness One dare not sound—

233

235

1072. A loss of something ever felt I—
1073. Herein a Blossom lies—
1074. What did They do since I saw Them?
1075. As plan for Noon and plan for Night
1076. Of Consciousness, her awful mate
1077. A Cloud withdrew from the Sky
1078. Of Silken Speech and Specious Shoe
1079. How fortunate the Grave—
1080. How happy I was if I could forget
1081. Experiment to me
1082. That Such have died enable Us
1083. Sang from the Heart, Sire,
1084. Fate slew Him, but He did not drop—
1085. Who is the East?
1086. Nature rarer uses Yellow
1087. To help our Bleaker Parts
1088. I've dropped my Brain—My Soul is numb—
1089. The Opening and the Close
1090. The quiet Dust was Gentlemen and Ladies
1091. To own the Art within the Soul
1092. There is a finished feeling
1093. 'Twas Crisis—All the length had passed—
1094. We outgrow love, like other things
1095. When I have seen the Sun emerge
1096. A narrow Fellow in the Grass
1097. Ashes denote that Fire was—
1098. The Leaves like Women, interchange
1099. At Half past Three
1100. The last Night that She lived
1101. If Nature smiles—the Mother must
1102. Dew—is the Freshet in the Grass—
1103. Perception of an Object costs
1104. The Crickets sang
1105. Of the Heart that goes in, and closes the Door
1106. These are the Signs to Nature's Inns—
1107. My Cocoon tightens—Colors teaze—
1108. The Bustle in a House
1109. The Sun went down—no Man looked on—
1110. One Day is there of the series
1111. He outstripped Time with but a Bout,
1112. This is a Blossom of the Brain—
1113. All Circumstances are the Frame
1114. A Shade opon the mind there passes
1115. It is an honorable Thought
1116. The Sunset stopped on Cottages
1117. Let down the Bars, Oh Death—
1118. Reportless Subjects, to the Quick
1119. Pain has but one Acquaintance
1120. Gratitude—is not the mention
1121. The Sky is low—the Clouds are mean.
1122. I cannot meet the Spring— unmoved—
1123. Between the form of Life and Life
1124. Count not that far that can be had
1125. Paradise is of the Option—
1126. His Bill is locked—his Eye estranged
1127. After the Sun comes out
1128. Distance—is not the Realm of Fox
1129. I fit for them—I seek the Dark
1130. The Frost of Death was on the Pane—

237

1195. Society for me my misery
1196. Safe Despair it is that raves—
1197. We never know how high we are
1198. This slow Day moved along—
1199. A soft Sea washed around the House
1200. Whatever it is—she has tried it—
1201. Too few the mornings be,
1202. Of so divine a Loss
1203. On the World you colored
1204. Lest they should come—is all my fear
1205. All men for Honor hardest work
1206. Of Paul and Silas it is said
1207. The Voice that stands for Floods to me
1208. "Remember Me" implored the Thief—
1209. Somehow myself survived the Night
1210. Some we see no more, Tenements of Wonder
1211. It's Hour with itself
1212. My Triumph lasted till the Drums
1213. Like Trains of Cars on Tracks of Plush
1214. Not any higher stands the Grave
1215. The harm of Years is on him—
1216. A Wind that rose though not a Leaf
1217. I worked for chaff and earning Wheat
1218. The Bone that has no Marrow,
1219. Who goes to dine must take his Feast
1220. The Popular Heart is a Cannon first—
1221. It came at last but prompter Death
1222. The pungent Atom in the Air
1223. Immortal is an ample word

1224. Are Friends Delight or Pain?
1225. The Mountains stood in Haze—
1226. Somewhere opon the general Earth
1227. Step lightly on this narrow Spot—
1228. I cannot want it more—
1229. The Days that we can spare
1230. 'Twas fighting for his Life he was—
1231. Frigid and sweet Her parting Face—
1232. An honest Tear
1233. I should not dare to be so sad
1234. Remembrance has a Rear and Front.
1235. Because my Brook is fluent
1236. A little Dog that wags his tail
1237. Oh Shadow on the Grass—
1238. To make Routine a Stimulus
1239. To disappear enhances—
1240. So much of Heaven has gone from Earth
1241. Like Brooms of Steel
1242. The Stars are old, that stood for me—
1243. Shall I take thee, the Poet said
1244. Fly—fly—but as you fly—
1245. Like Rain it sounded till it curved
1246. The Clouds their Backs together laid
1247. We like a Hairbreadth 'scape
1248. The Sun and Fog contested
1249. Had I not seen the Sun
1250. If my Bark sink
1251. Look back on Time, with kindly Eyes—
1252. It is the Meek that Valor wear
1253. Risk is the Hair that holds the Tun
1254. Let my first knowing be of thee
1255. Fortitude incarnate
1256. A Clover's simple Fame

1390. Take all away—

1391. I sued the News—yet feared—the News

1392. Love's stricken "why"

1393. Those Cattle smaller than a Bee

1394. The long sigh of the Frog

1395. The Butterfly's Numidian Gown

1396. Of his peculiar light

1397. How firm eternity must look

1398. Gathered into the Earth,

1399. The Sun is one—and on the Tare

1400. The worthlessness of Earthly things

1401. Dreams are the subtle Dower

1402. His Heart was darker than the starless night

1403. Touch lightly Nature's sweet Guitar

1404. In many and reportless places

1405. Long Years apart—can make no

1406. Praise it—'tis dead—

1407. A Saucer holds a Cup

1408. The Bat is dun, with wrinkled Wings—

1409. Death warrants are supposed to be

1410. The Flake the Wind exasperate

1411. Summer laid her simple Hat

1412. How know it from a Summer's Day?

1413. Summer—we all have seen—

1414. How fits his Umber Coat

1415. Trusty as the stars

1416. These held their Wick above the west—

1417. "Tomorrow"—whose location

1418. A wild Blue sky abreast of Winds

1419. A—Field of Stubble, lying sere

1420. How much the present moment means

1421. Of Paradise' existence

1422. March is the Month of Expectation.

1423. The inundation of the Spring

1424. Hope is a strange invention—

1425. They might not need me—yet they might.

1426. Bees are Black—with Gilt Surcingles—

1427. Whose Pink career may have a close

1428. Lay this Laurel on the one

1429. I shall not murmur if at last

1430. We shun because we prize her Face

1431. Such are the inlets of the mind—

1432. I have no Life but this—

1433. What mystery pervades a well!

1434. To the stanch Dust

1435. The Fact that Earth is Heaven—

1436. To own a Susan of my own

1437. Shame is the shawl of Pink

1438. Sweet skepticism of the Heart—

1439. Unworthy of her Breast

1440. How Human Nature dotes

1441. How lonesome the Wind must feel Nights—

1442. It was a quiet seeming Day—

1443. The fairest Home I ever knew

1444. The pretty Rain from those sweet Eaves

1445. To earn it by disdaining it

1446. Water makes many Beds

1447. Who never wanted—maddest Joy

1448. With Pinions of Disdain

1449. Ourselves—we do inter—with sweet derision

1450. One Joy of so much anguish

1451. No Passenger was known to flee—

1514. A Counterfeit—a Plated Person—

1515. Estranged from Beauty—none can be—

1516. One thing of thee I covet—

1517. We shall find the Cube of the Rainbow—

1518. Glass was the Street—in Tinsel Peril

1519. It came his turn to beg—

1520. The Robin is a Gabriel

1521. The Face in Evanescence lain

1522. A Dimple in the Tomb

1523. How soft a Caterpillar steps—

1524. Could that sweet Darkness where they dwell

1525. The Road to Paradise is plain—

1526. Love is done when Love's begun,

1527. Her spirit rose to such a hight

1528. The Thrill came slowly like a Boon for

1529. All that I do

1530. Facts by our side are never sudden

1531. I saw the wind within her—

1532. More than the Grave is closed to me—

1533. Of whom so dear

1534. I do not care—why should I care

1535. She could not live upon the Past

1536. You cannot make Remembrance grow

1537. "And with what Body do they come"?

1538. The Savior must have been

1539. Mine Enemy is growing old—

1540. My country need not change her gown,

1541. Birthday of but a single pang

1542. Drowning is not so pitiful

1543. The Stem of a departed Flower

1544. An Antiquated Tree

1545. A Pang is more conspicuous in Spring

1546. We never know we go when we are going—

1547. The Bumble Bee's Religion—

1548. All things swept sole away

1549. A faded Boy—in sallow Clothes

1550. Oh give it motion—deck it sweet

1551. 'Tis Seasons since the Dimpled War

1552. Above Oblivion's Tide there is a Pier

1553. From all the Jails the Boys and Girls

1554. On that specific Pillow

1555. The Life that tied too tight escapes

1556. The Bird her punctual music brings

1557. How fleet—how indiscreet an one—

1558. The Blood is more showy than the Breath

1559. The Butterfly upon the Sky

1560. There comes a warning like a spy

1561. "Go traveling with us"!

1562. His oriental heresies

1563. No Autumn's intercepting Chill

1564. The Things that never can come back, are several—

1565. The Dandelion's pallid Tube

1566. Not seeing, still we know—

1567. How much of Source escapes with thee—

1568. Sweet Pirate of the Heart,

1569. Echo has no Magistrate—

1570. How happy is the little Stone

1571. He lived the Life of Ambush

1572. Come show thy Durham Breast

1573. Obtaining but our own extent
1574. The Moon upon her fluent Route
1575. Now I lay thee down to Sleep—
1576. No matter where the Saints abide,
1577. The Bible is an antique Volume—
1578. Meeting by Accident,
1579. My Wars are laid away in Books—
1580. The pattern of the sun
1581. Those—dying then,
1582. Within thy Grave!
1583. Bliss is the sceptre of the child
1584. "Go tell it"—What a Message—
1585. I groped for him before I knew
1586. Image of Light, Adieu—
1587. Lives he in any other world
1588. Of Death I try to think like this,
1589. Tried always and Condemned by thee
1590. Elysium is as far as to
1591. If I should see a single bird
1592. Cosmopolites without a plea
1593. He ate and drank the precious Words—
1594. Pompless no Life can pass away—
1595. We shun it ere it comes,
1596. No Brigadier throughout the Year
1597. To see her is a Picture—
1598. The Clock strikes One
1599. A Sloop of Amber slips away
1600. Forever honored by the Tree
1601. To be forgot by thee
1602. His Losses made our Gains ashamed—
1603. To the bright east she flies,
1604. Not at Home to Callers
1605. No ladder needs the bird but skies

1606. Lad of Athens, faithful be
1607. How slow the Wind—how slow the Sea—
1608. Candor—my tepid friend—
1609. Who has not found the Heaven—below—
1610. Where Roses would not dare to go
1611. By homely gifts and hindered words
1612. Witchcraft was hung, in History,
1613. The Lassitudes of Contemplation
1614. Blossoms will run away—
1615. It would not know if it were spurned,
1616. This Me—that walks and works—must die
1617. To her derided Home
1618. There came a Wind like a Bugle—
1619. We wear our sober Dresses when we die,
1620. The Bobolink is gone—the Rowdy of the Meadow—
1621. Morning is due to all—
1622. The Summer that we did not prize
1623. The Heart has many Doors—
1624. Pass to thy Rendezvous of Light,
1625. Expanse cannot be lost—
1626. Climbing to reach the costly Hearts
1627. The Spirit lasts—but in what mode—
1628. Immured in Heaven!
1629. To try to speak, and miss the way
1630. A Drunkard cannot meet a Cork
1631. 'Tis not the swaying frame we miss—
1632. Quite empty, quite at rest,
1633. Within that little Hive
1634. Each that we lose takes part of us;

1635. Arrows enamored of his Heart—

1636. Circumference thou Bride of Awe

1637. There are two Mays

1638. Declaiming Waters none may dread—

1639. Few, yet enough,

1640. Who is it seeks my Pillow Nights,

1641. Though the great Waters sleep,

1642. A World made penniless by that departure

1643. We send the wave to find the wave,

1644. Sunset that screens, reveals—

1645. Morning, that comes but once,

1646. The Auctioneer of Parting

1647. Not knowing when the Dawn will come,

1648. A Flower will not trouble her, it has so small a Foot,

1649. Back from the Cordial Grave I drag thee

1650. The Pedigree of Honey

1651. As from the Earth the light Balloon

1652. Oh Future! thou secreted peace

1653. So give me back to Death—

1654. Still own thee—still thou art

1655. Talk not to me of Summer Trees

1656. The Sun in reining to the West

1657. Betrothed to Righteousness might be

1658. Show me Eternity, and I will show you Memory—

1659. I held it so tight that I lost it

1660. But that defeated accent

1661. Not Sickness stains the Brave,

1662. The going from a world we know

1663. Upon his Saddle sprung a Bird

1664. In other Motes,

1665. The farthest Thunder that I heard

1666. Some Arrows slay but whom they strike,

1667. Parting with Thee reluctantly,

1668. Apparently with no surprise

1669. Oh what a Grace is this—

1670. The Jay his Castanet has struck

1671. Take all away from me, but leave me Ecstasy,

1672. A Letter is a joy of Earth—

1673. Go thy great way!

1674. Is it too late to touch you, Dear?

1675. Of God we ask one favor, that we may be forgiven—

1676. A chastened Grace is twice a Grace—

1677. Their dappled importunity

1678. Some one prepared this mighty show

1679. The Ditch is dear to the Drunken man

1680. The Ecstasy to guess,

1681. "Red Sea," indeed! Talk not to me

1682. Extol thee—could I—Then I will

1683. Why should we hurry—Why indeed

1684. The immortality she gave

1685. Of Glory not a Beam is left

1686. The gleam of an heroic act

1687. Beauty crowds me till I die

1688. Endanger it, and the Demand

1689. To tell the Beauty would decrease

1690. The Blunder is in estimate

1691. Volcanoes be in Sicily

1692. Of this is Day composed

1693. Summer begins to have the look

1694. Speech is one symptom of affection

1695. I see thee clearer for the Grave

1766. The waters chased him as he fled,
1767. The words the happy say
1768. There comes an hour when begging
      stops,
1769. This docile one inter
1770. Through those old grounds of
      memory,
1771. 'Twas here my summer paused
1772. Softened by Time's consummate plush,
1773. My life closed twice before it's close;
1774. A face devoid of love or grace,
1775. Upon the gallows hung a wretch,
1776. The reticent volcano keeps
1777. To lose thee—sweeter than to gain
1778. High from the earth I heard a bird;
1779. To make a prairie it takes a clover
      and one bee,
1780. Sweet is the swamp with it's secrets,
1781. The distance that the dead have gone
1782. How dare the robins sing,
1783. Death is like the insect
1784. The grave my little cottage is,
1785. Sweet hours have perished here,
1786. Which misses most—
1787. Were nature mortal lady
1788. Fame is a bee.
1789. The saddest noise, the sweetest noise,

ABOUT THE AUTHOR

Paul Legault is the author of two previous books of
poetry: *The Madeleine Poems* (Omnidawn, 2010) and
The Other Poems (Fence, 2011). He is the co-founder of
the translation press Telephone Books, and an editor of
The Sonnets: Translating and Rewriting Shakespeare, 154
poets' take on the bard's own. He lives in Brooklyn.